MATHS
IN ACTION
PLUS

AUTHORS

R. Howat Adviser, Ayr
G. Marra Linlathen High School, Dundee
E. Mullan Galashiels Academy
R. Murray Hawick High School
J. Thomson Galashiels Academy

STUDENTS' BOOK

Thomas Nelson and Sons Ltd
Nelson House Mayfield Road
Walton-on-Thames Surrey
KT12 5PL UK

Thomas Nelson Australia
102 Dodds Street
South Melbourne
Victoria 3205 Australia

Nelson Canada
1120 Birchmount Road
Scarborough Ontario
MIK 5G4 Canada

Cover photograph courtesy of Rutherford Appleton Laboratory

First published by Thomas Nelson and Sons Ltd 1997
I ⓣ P Thomas Nelson is an International Thomson Publishing Company
I ⓣ P is used under licence

ISBN 0–17–431458–2
NPN 9 8 7 6 5 4 3 2 1

Printed in China.

CONTENTS

Note: the 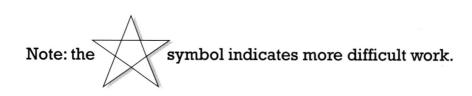 symbol indicates more difficult work.

1 COORDINATES

LOOKING BACK

1 Kirsty is on the third floor
at window D.
We say she is at **D3**.

At which window
can you see:

a a plant
b a Christmas tree
c a television
d a lamp?

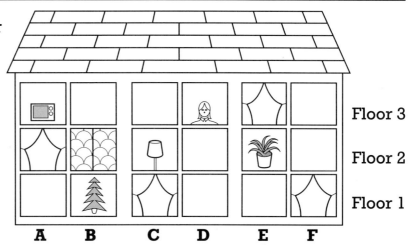

Floor 3

Floor 2

Floor 1

A B C D E F

2 Granny Smith planted apple trees in
her orchard.
They were planted in neat rows.

Some of the trees died, leaving gaps
in the rows.

a Give the position of the tree which
has lots of apples on it.
b Write down the positions of the dead trees.
c Apple trees cost £8 each.
How much will it cost to replace
the dead trees?

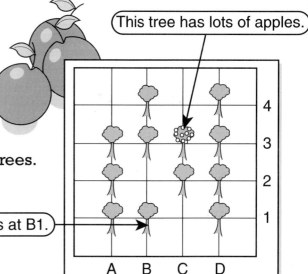

This tree has lots of apples.

This tree is at B1.

3

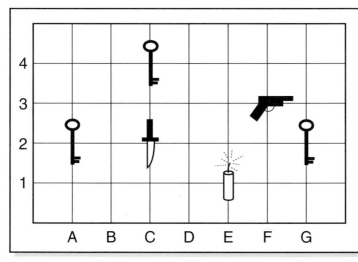

Ivan is playing a game on
his computer.

The stick of dynamite is
at E1.

a Where is the gun?
b What is at C2?
c Three keys are on
the screen.
Where are they?

Coordinates

Up

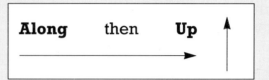

Remember

Each point on the grid can be found by giving two instructions.

| **Along** | then | **Up** ↑ |

→

A is the point (3, 2).
To find A, move **along** 3 then **up** 2.

B is the point (2, 4).
To find B, move **along** 2 then **up** 4.

Along

Start

EXERCISE 1

1 Inverness is at (4, 5) on the grid.

  a Which town is at (6, 2)?
  b What is the position of Ullapool?
  c Name the other three towns on the map. Give their positions on the grid.

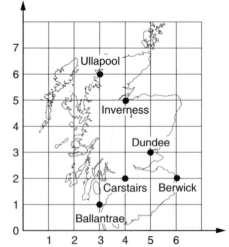

2 This computer game shows animals on a grid.

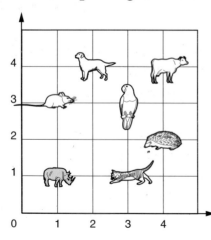

The rhinoceros is at (1, 1).

  a Where is the cat?
  b Which animal is at (4, 2)?
  c What is the position of the parrot?
  d Write down the position of the mouse.
  e Which animal is at (4, 4) on the grid?

Do Worksheet **1**

2

3 This grid shows a treasure map.

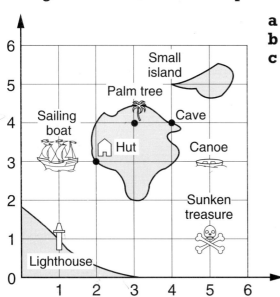

a What is the position of the sailing boat?
b What is at (3, 4)?
c Write down the position of the:
  (i) cave
  (ii) sunken treasure
  (iii) canoe
  (iv) lighthouse
  (v) hut.

4 The seas round the island are dangerous.
The dotted lines show safe routes.
We can use coordinates to describe
these routes.

Example:
(4, 5)→(3, 6)→(1, 5)→(0, 3)→(1, 1)
takes you from the small island
to the lighthouse.

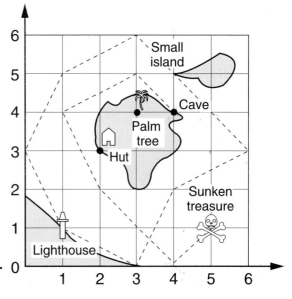

a (i) Describe the other safe route from
    the small island to the lighthouse.
  (ii) Describe the safe route from
    the cave to the sunken treasure.
b Describe the following routes in words.
  (i) (4, 5)→(4, 4)
  (ii) (4, 4)→(5, 3)→(5, 1)→(1, 1)

5

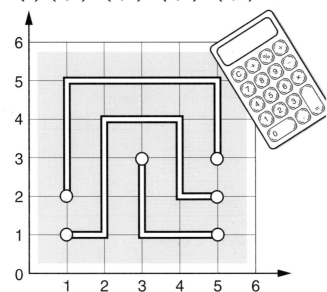

The grid shows a printed circuit
inside a calculator.

Use coordinates to describe the
track which joins:

a (1, 1) to (5, 2)

b (1, 2) to (5, 3)

c (5, 1) to (3, 3)

Plotting Points

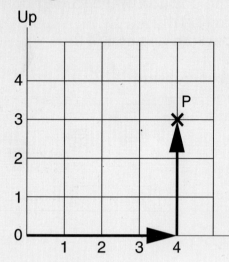

Up

Along

Example

On the grid, mark P(4, 3).

Start at 0.

Move along 4, then up 3.

Put a small cross.
Write **P** next to the cross.

EXERCISE 2

You will need a Grid Sheet (or squared paper).

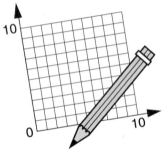

1 Plot these points on a grid:

   A (4, 1)   B (2, 5)   C (6, 6)   D (7, 0)   E (9, 8)

   F (1, 3)   G (10, 10) H (0, 5)   I (3, 7)   J (8, 1)

   K (5, 9) L (8, 8)   M (4, 8) N (0, 7) O (0, 0)

2 a (i) Plot these points, joining them as you plot:
    P(1, 2)→Q(6, 2)→R(6, 5)→S(1, 5)→P.
  (ii) What shape have you drawn?

  b (i) Plot and join these points:
    D(1, 4)→E(3, 6)→F(7, 4)→G(3, 2)→D.
  (ii) What shape is DEFG?

3 a (i) Plot and join these points: A(0, 6)→B(6, 6)→C(6, 1).
  (ii) ABCD is a rectangle. Where is D?

  b (i) On the same grid as above,
    plot and join these points:
    P(2, 0)→Q(2, 3)→R(7, 3)→S(7, 0)→P.
  (ii) PQRS meets ABCD at two places.
    Give their coordinates.

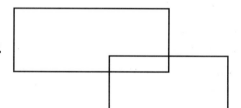

Magic Mirrors

We can change a drawing by
putting it on a different grid.

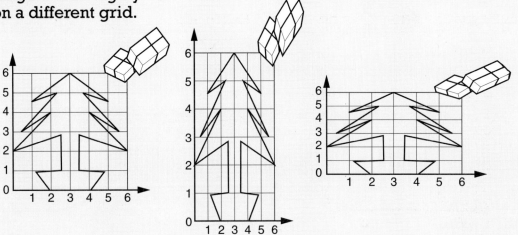

EXERCISE 3

You will need a Magic Mirror Grid Sheet.

1 Plot these points on the first grid on the sheet.
Join them up in order, as you go along.

(1, 6)	(2, 9)	(3, 10)	(4, 10)	(4, 11)	(3, 12)	(3, 13)
(4, 14)	(5, 14)	(6, 13)	(6, 12)	(5, 11)	(5, 10)	(6, 10)
(7, 9)	(8, 6)	(7, 6)	(6, 9)	(6, 2)	(7, 2)	(7, 1)
(5, 1)	(5, 5)	(4, 5)	(4, 1)	(2, 1)	(2, 2)	(3, 2)

(3, 9) (2, 6) and back to (1, 6)

2 Choose one of the other grids and draw this picture again.
How has the grid changed your picture?

3 On the other grids,
> **either** draw this shape again
> **or** use the instructions on More Practice 3
> to draw more distorted pictures.

4 Make a wall display with your best distorted pictures.

5 a Explore how you can change the shapes of letters by
this method.

A   A   A   ⌒

b Examine the bar code on the right. What is it?

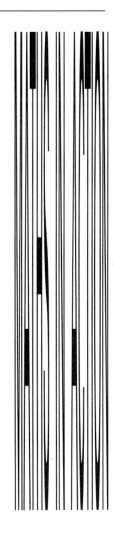

5

Proper Names

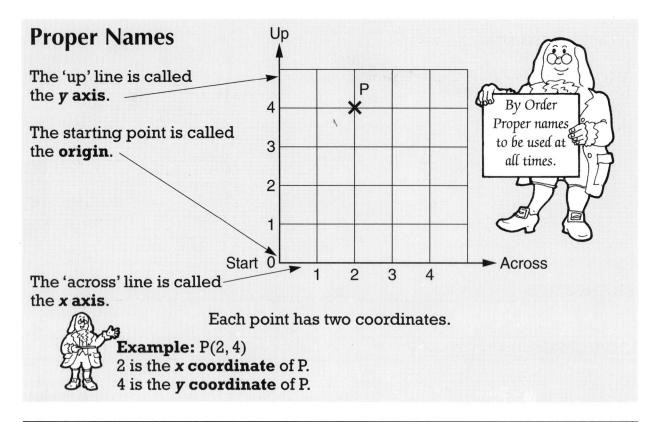

The 'up' line is called the **y axis**.

The starting point is called the **origin**.

The 'across' line is called the **x axis**.

By Order
Proper names
to be used at
all times.

Each point has two coordinates.

Example: P(2, 4)
2 is the **x coordinate** of P.
4 is the **y coordinate** of P.

EXERCISE 4

1 List all the points in the diagram. Write down their coordinates.

Use your list to answer these questions about the points.

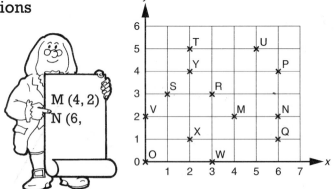

M (4, 2)
N (6,

2 The x coordinate of M is 4.
What is the x coordinate of P?

3 The y coordinate of T is 5.
What is the y coordinate of R?

4 Which **two** points have the same x coordinate as N?

5 Which point has the same y coordinate as the point X?

6 Some points have the same number for their x coordinate and their y coordinate. Which points are these?

7 Which points are on the x axis?

8 a What do you call the point where the x axis and the y axis meet?
   b What are the coordinates of this point?

9 Four points on the grid can be joined to make a rectangle. Name them.

⭐ Extending the Grid

We can show we have gone **below** the *x* axis
by using a **negative**.

Example

B is the point (4, –2).
Along 4, then **down** 2.

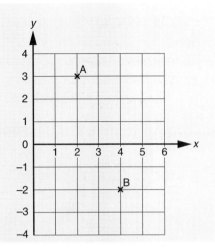

EXERCISE 5

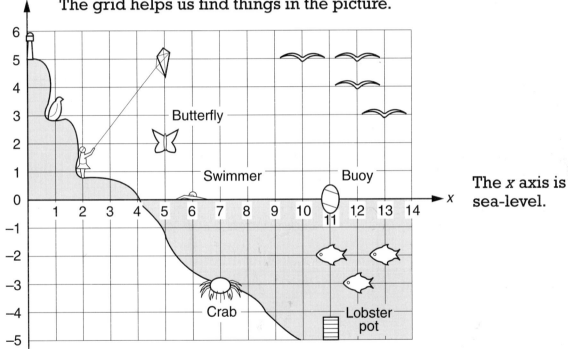

This picture shows some cliffs, the sea and the sky.
The grid helps us find things in the picture.

The *x* axis is sea-level.

1 One of the seagulls is at (13, 3). What are the coordinates of the other three?

2 Write down the coordinates of the swimmer.

3 One fish is at (11, –2). Write down the coordinates of the other two fish.

4 A bird is sitting on a nest on the cliff. What are the coordinates of the nest?

5 A crab is crawling along the seabed. What are the coordinates of the crab?

6 Write down the coordinates of:
   a the woman   **b** the lobster pot   **c** the kite   **d** the buoy   **e** the butterfly.

⭐ Extending the Grid Further

We can show we have gone backwards
   behind the *y* axis
      by using a **negative**.

Examples

C is the point (–2, 3).
Back 2, then up 3.

D is the point (–4, –2).
Back 4, then **down** 2.

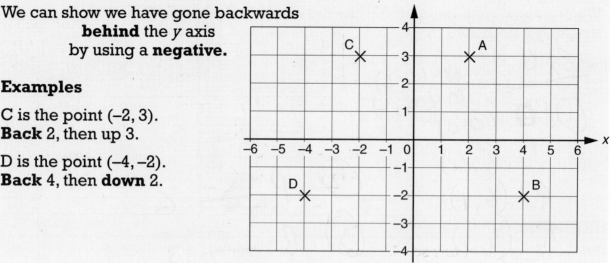

7 The picture shows a radar display at an airport.

The airport is at (0, 0).

Each cross is an aeroplane.

P is (3, 2).
R is (–5, 3).

Give the coordinates of
all the other planes.

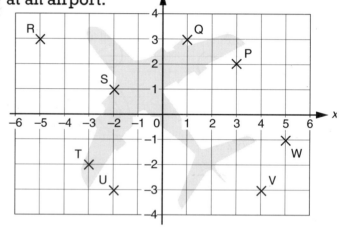

8 There is a map in the Fun Park to help you find your way.

The map is at (0, 0). (You are here.)

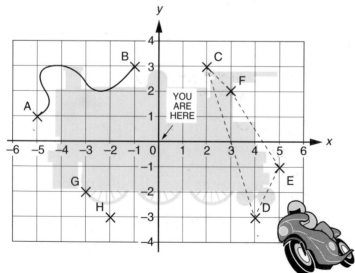

a The roller coaster runs
from A to B.
Give the coordinates of
both points.

b The scenic railway follows
the route C→D→E→F→C.
Describe the route using
coordinates.

c G and H are entrances to
the café.
Give their coordinates.

d The Wall of Death ride
starts at (–5, –1). Which
point already mentioned is
nearest to it?

CHECK-UP ON COORDINATES

1 Hawick Academy is putting on a pantomime. The plan shows the seating arrangement in the hall.

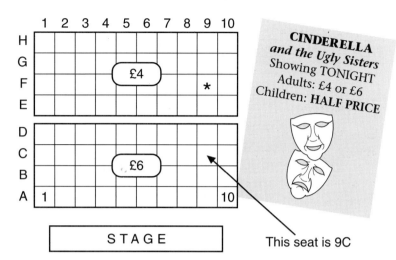

CINDERELLA
and the Ugly Sisters
Showing TONIGHT
Adults: £4 or £6
Children: HALF PRICE

This seat is 9C

a One of the seats is marked with a star, *. What is the number of the seat?

b Mr and Mrs MacKenzie sit in seats 3C and 4C. How much will the tickets cost altogether?

c Jan Evans and her son Herman (age 10) sit in seats 7E and 8E. How much will their tickets cost?

2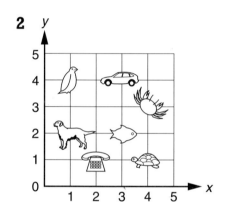

a What is at (3, 4)?

b What are the coordinates of:
(i) the telephone
(ii) the crab?

c Which item is closest to:
(i) (0, 2)   (ii) (4, 0)?

3 Copy this grid onto squared paper.

a Plot the points P(1, 1), Q(1, 4) and R(5, 4).

b Find S so that PQRS is a rectangle. Mark S on your grid.

c Write down the coordinates of S.

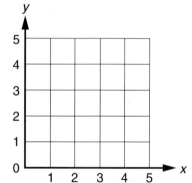

4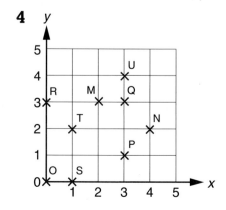

a Which point on the grid has a y coordinate of 1?

b Which point has an x coordinate of 2?

c One point apart from O has the same number for its x and y coordinate. Which point is it?

d Which point is on the y axis?

e What is the name given to the point marked O?

2 PROPORTION

LOOKING BACK

1 a In the China Bazaar, cups and
saucers are priced as shown.
   (i)   How much will it cost
         for six cups?
   (ii) How much will ten
         saucers cost?

**Bargain prices
Beautiful porcelain**

Cups   £2.00 each
Saucers   £1.50 each

Winter Green Plates
4 for £8.00

b Four plates cost £8.
   (i)   What does one plate cost?
   (ii) How much will 12 plates cost?

2 There are 48 hours in two days.

NEWSFLASH! **48-hour flu hits factory**

a How many hours make one day?

b A common cold lasts for five days.
   How many hours is this?

3

a A model of the Jupiter Jet is 30 cm long.
   The real thing is **20 times** longer.
   How long is the actual Jet?

b The model racing car is 8 cm long.
   The real car is 400 cm long.
   What does 1 cm on the model stand for?

4

Pancake Mix
Makes enough for 15 pancakes

Flour	100 g
Eggs	1
Milk	250 ml
Fat	50 g

Mrs Mills is cooking for a sale of work.
She has to make 60 pancakes.

a Write out the ingredients she needs.

b To save money she uses a mix of half
   milk and half water instead of milk.
   How much water will she need for:
   (i)   15 pancakes
   (ii) 60 pancakes?

Rates Tell You About One

Example

Laura types at a rate of 40 words per minute.
How many words can she type in 8 minutes?

She types 40 words in **one** minute.
40 × 8 = 320
Laura can type 320 words in 8 minutes.

EXERCISE 1

1 David types at a rate of 45 words per minute.

How many words can he type in 6 minutes?

2  Ice-cream cones
cost 80 pence each.

What is the cost
of 5 cones?

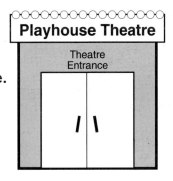

3 It costs £5 per person to get into the theatre.

What is the cost for 6 people?

4  The lorry travels at 60 kilometres per hour.

How far will it travel in 4 hours?

5 Joyce's car travels 36 miles
per gallon of petrol used.

How far will she travel on 4 gallons?

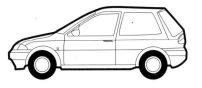

6  Jafar's heart beats at the rate of 84 beats per minute.

How many beats will it make in 5 minutes?

7 Andrew works in a bakery.
He is paid £2.80 per hour.

a He works four hours per night.
How much does he earn in a night?

b He works 16 hours a week.
How much is he paid per week?

8

Don't be a drip!
Get your taps fixed.
A dripping tap can
lose 10 litres a day.

a How much water could be lost
in a 7-day week?

b How much water could be lost in
a year if the tap is not fixed?

9 Jim is on a long hike.
He aims to travel 80 km per day.

How far does he aim to go in
5 days?

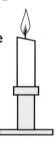

10

Ruth works in a soft-toy factory.
She puts the finishing touches to the elephants.
Her target is 12 elephants per hour.

a What is her target for an 8-hour day?

b She works a 37-hour week.
How many elephants should she be able to finish?

11 In experiments, Julie found that a candle
burned at the rate of 1.5 cm per hour.

A candle lasted 8 hours.

What length of candle was it?

12 It costs £200 a day to go on a cruise on the *Queen Matilda*.

a How much does a 7-day
cruise cost?

b Janet paid £1800 for a cruise.
How many days did she pay for?

Finding the Rate

Example

Walter is paid £28 for working 7 hours.
What is his rate of pay per hour?

'Pay per hour' means pay ÷ hours.
28 ÷ 7 = 4
Walter gets £4 per hour.

per means ÷

EXERCISE 2

1  Mike takes 60 minutes to read 5 pages of a book.

Work out his reading rate in **minutes per page.**

2 Joe can type 168 words in 4 minutes.
Work out his typing rate in **words per minute.**

3 A digger can make a drainage trench 800 cm long
in 40 minutes.
What is the digger's rate of work in **centimetres per minute?**

4 Nicola's heart beats 264 times in 3 minutes.
What is her heart rate in **beats per minute?**

5 Seven pens are bought for £3.57.

Work out the rate at which the pens are sold in **pence per pen.**

6 A jet can cover a distance of 2436 miles in 3.5 hours.
What is its rate of travel in **miles per hour?**

7 Ten people went to a pantomime.
It cost a total of £45 for them to get in.
What is the rate charged by the theatre in **pounds per person?**

8 10 litres of paint cover 406 square metres of wall.
What area will 1 litre cover?
Write your answer as a rate.

Work out the Rate First

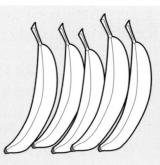

Example

Three bananas cost 93 pence.
What is the cost of five bananas?

Work out the cost per banana.
93 ÷ 3 = 31 pence per banana
So five bananas cost 5 × 31 = 155 pence.

EXERCISE 3

1  Seven apples cost 84 pence.

    a Work out the rate in pence per apple.
    b What is the cost of nine apples?

2 3 kg of potatoes cost £1.20.

    a Work out the rate in pounds (£) per kilogram.
    b What is the cost of 2 kg?

3 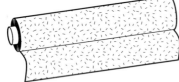 2 m of curtain material cost £7.00.

    a Work out the rate in pounds (£) per metre.
    b What is the cost of 10 m of the material?

4 Jack drives 400 km in five hours.

    a Work out his rate of travel **(km per hour)**.
    b How far would he drive in seven hours?

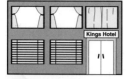

5 Paula paid £22 for 40 litres of petrol.
How much would a full tank of 47 litres cost her?

6 A hotel charged £81 for a stay of three nights.
How much would they charge for five nights?

7 Seven people paid a total of £24.50 to see the film *Viking Raiders*.
How much would it cost for a party of nine?

8 On holiday in Greece, Lucy changed £3 for 960 drachmas.
How many drachmas would she get for £5?

9 Charles was paid £44.80 for 16 hours of work.
How much would he be paid for working 12 hours?

10 £10 can be exchanged for 95 French francs.
How many francs can you get for £101?

11 Four tins of Top Kat last Felix seven days.
How long will 12 tins last?

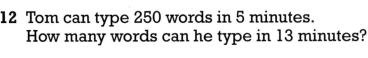

12 Tom can type 250 words in 5 minutes.
How many words can he type in 13 minutes?

13  It takes Alan 3 hours to paint
an area of 45 square metres.
What area can he paint in 2.5 hours?

Do Worksheet **1**

 ## Working out the Best Buy

Work out what you get for 1p. The bigger your answer, the better the buy.

Example

100 g of Top Blend coffee cost £2.50. $100 \div 250 = 0.4$ g per 1p.
200 g of Top Blend coffee cost £4.50. $200 \div 450 =$ **0.444 g** per 1p.

Which is the better buy?   The 200 g jar is the better buy.

EXERCISE 4

Work out the better buy in each case.

1 Aromatic Coffee   100 g for £2.40   **or** Breakfast Coffee   175 g for £4.00

2 Choco Bar   175 g for £2.38   **or** Dairy Crunch   300 g for £4.00

3 Exotic Peaches   220 g for 35p   **or** Flavourite Peaches   420 g for 60p

4 Green Tea   100 bags for £2.20   **or** Heavenly Bru   25 bags for £0.60

5   Which is the better buy here?
                         (Take care with the kilograms.)

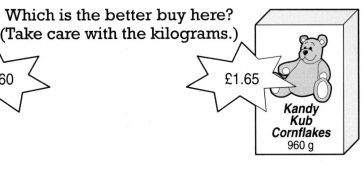

£5.60

£1.65

Jumping Jack Cornflakes 3.2 kg

Kandy Kub Cornflakes 960 g

Do Worksheet **2**

Mixing Parts

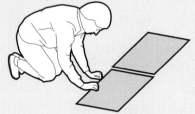

Jake mixes sand and cement to make a patio. He uses:
1 part sand and 3 parts of cement.

This means that, to make his mix,
for every **shovelful** of sand he uses he must use
3 shovelfuls of cement,
for every **barrowload** of sand he must use
3 barrowloads of cement,
for every **kilogram** of sand he must use
3 kilograms of cement.

When he uses **5 kg** of sand, he must use **3 × 5 kg = 15 kg** of cement.

EXERCISE 5

1. Green is a mix of
1 part blue to 2 parts yellow.

Copy and complete the table.

Blue	Yellow
1 ml	2 ml
2 ml	4 ml
3 ml	
6 ml	
	50 ml

2. To make an undercoat mix I use
1 part paint to 4 parts water.

Copy and complete the table.

Paint	Water
1 ml	4 ml
20 ml	80 ml
300 ml	
6 litres	
	40 ml

3.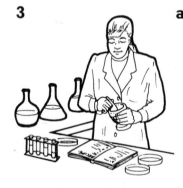

   a. A chemist reads this in an old recipe book:
   'To make peppermint water, use **1 teaspoon of essence with 3 cups of water**.'

   Copy and complete the table.

Essence	Water
1 spoon	3 cups
2 spoons	6 cups
5 spoons	
10 spoons	
	18 cups

   b. She also reads this: 'To make face toner, use **1 part of witch-hazel to 2 parts of rosewater**.'

   Copy and complete the table.

Witch-hazel	Rosewater
1 part	2 parts
2 cups	4 cups
5 cups	
10 ml	
	100 ml

c  Finally, she reads this:
'To make bath oil, use the oils of rose, lavender and geranium.
Use **1 measure of lavender** with **2 measures of rose** and **5 measures of geranium**.'

She uses 2 measures of lavender for a batch.
How many measures of:
(i)   rose
(ii) geranium are needed?
(iii) Copy and complete the table.

| Measures of | | |
Lavender	Rose	Geranium
1	2	5
2		
6		
	8	
		25

EXERCISE 6

1 Mrs Williams makes Christmas cakes as presents.

Her recipe for **one** cake is:
300 g of flour
200 g of butter
200 g of sugar
4 eggs
125 ml of milk
900 g of mixed fruit.

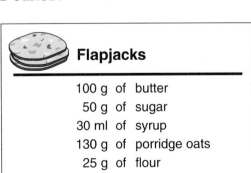

a List the ingredients she needs for four cakes.

b She buys 18 eggs.
Is this enough for four cakes?

c She measures out 1 kg of flour.
How much **more** does she need for four cakes?

2 Mrs Williams also makes flapjacks.
This recipe will make 20 flapjacks.

a List the ingredients for 60 flapjacks.

b How much sugar is needed for 10 flapjacks?

c How many flapjacks will she make if she uses:
(i)   200 g of butter
(ii) 150 g of butter?

Flapjacks

100 g of butter
50 g of sugar
30 ml of syrup
130 g of porridge oats
25 g of flour

3

GILBERT'S GARDEN CENTRE
You need the right mix for the job.

	Peat	Sand	Soil
For seeds	2	1	6
For flowers	2	1	5
For shrubs	4	0	1

a Mr Green wants to make a mixture for seeds.
The table tells him 2 parts peat, 1 part sand and 6 parts soil.
He uses 10 pots of sand.

How many pots does he need of:
(i)   peat   (ii) soil?

b He makes a mixture to pot shrubs.
He uses 20 pots of peat.

Work out the rest of the mixture.

4 The amount of water you add to each packet of wallpaper paste depends on the type of wallpaper you use.

a Tessa Walls uses two packets of paste to make a mixture for normal paper.

How much water does she need?

For 1 packet paper type	Quantity of cold water
Normal Paper	6 litres
Washable and Vinyls	5 litres
Woodchip	4 litres
Heavy Embossed	3.5 litres

b Three packets of paste are used to do a job with heavy embossed paper.

How much water is needed?

c 16 litres of water were used to make a mix for woodchip.

How many packets of paste were needed?

Do Worksheet **3**

Gradients

 Road signs like this warn drivers of steep hills.
1:5 tells us that for every
5 metres that we go along the road
we climb 1 metre.

'We climb 1 metre in 5.'

EXERCISE 7

1  Copy and complete:

1:10 tells us that for every
... metres that we go along the road
we climb ... metre.

'We climb ... metre in ...'

2 Make similar statements about the following signs.

a    **b**    **c**    **d**

3 Here are some measurements taken along a 2:7 hill.

Copy and complete the table.

Metres up	Metres along
2	7
4	14
6	**a**
16	**b**
c	28
d	35

⭐ Graphs in Proportion

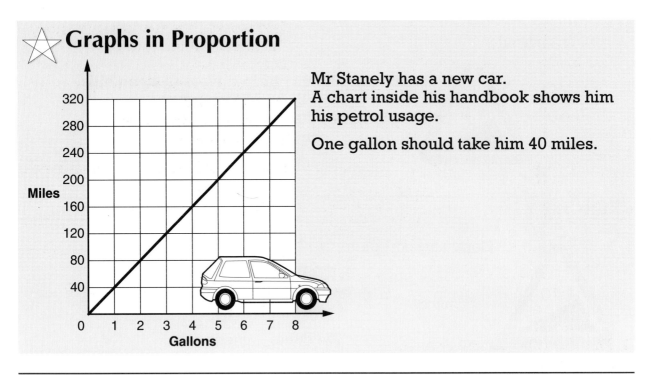

Mr Stanely has a new car.
A chart inside his handbook shows him his petrol usage.

One gallon should take him 40 miles.

EXERCISE 8

1 Use the above chart to answer these questions.

  a How many miles should Mr Stanely travel on:
     (i) 8 gallons   (ii) 2 gallons?

  b How much petrol should he need for a journey of 200 miles?

  c Mr Stanely wants to visit his sister who lives 280 miles away.
     His petrol gauge shows he has one gallon in his tank.
     What is the least amount of petrol he should buy?

2

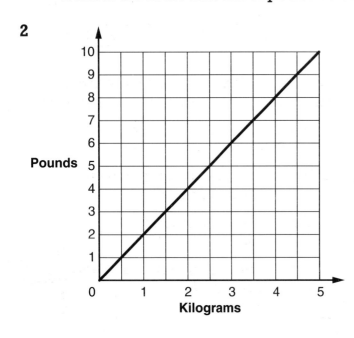

As a very rough guide,
1 kg = 2 pounds weight.

  a How many pounds make:

     (i)   3 kg   (ii) 5 kg
     (iii) 2.5 kg?

  b How many kilograms make:

     (i)   2 pounds   (ii) 8 pounds
     (iii) 9 pounds?

3

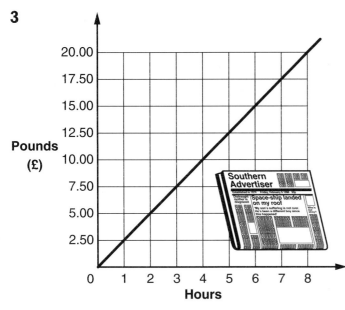

Kate works in a newsagent's shop.
She is paid at the rate of
£2.50 per hour.
The chart shows what wages
she can expect.
Use the chart to answer
these questions.

a How much money will she earn
for working:
(i)   0 hours   (ii)   1 hour
(iii)   3 hours?

b How many hours must she work
to earn:
(i)   £15   (ii)   £12.50
(iii)   £20?

4 This chart helps you to change
from inches to centimetres.

a How many centimetres make:
(i)   2 inches   (ii)   6 inches
(iii)   9 inches?

b How many inches make:
(i)   10 cm   (ii)   20 cm
(iii)   2.5 cm?

c An old DIY book says that
20 inches of beading are
required for a job.
How many centimetres
of beading are needed?

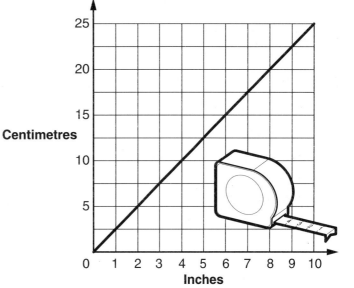

5

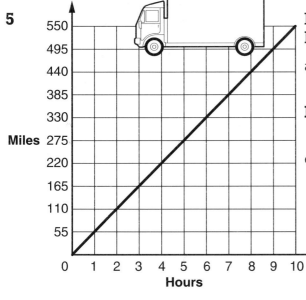

Paul drives his lorry down the motorway.
He can't go faster than 55 miles per hour.

a What is the farthest he can travel in:
(i)   2 hours   (ii)   9 hours?

b How long does he take to travel
385 miles at 55 mph?

c He wants to make a trip of
300 miles.

Can he do it in five hours?
(Give a reason for
your answer.)

Do
Worksheet
4

CHECK -UP ON PROPORTION

1 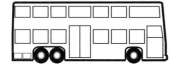 The Eastlands Bus Company charges 45 pence per kilometre.

   a What is the charge for a 7 kilometre journey?
   b How long is a journey that costs £9 (900p)?

2 At the butcher's, 5 kg of meat cost £18.00.

   How much will you pay for 7 kg of the same meat?

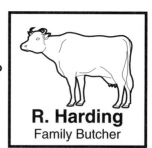

R. Harding
Family Butcher

3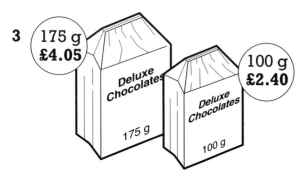

175 g
£4.05

100 g
£2.40

Susie wants to buy some chocolates.

Which is the better buy?

4 In the winter, Azra puts anti-freeze in her windscreen washer.
It is a mix of 1 part anti-freeze to 3 parts water.

Copy and complete the table.

Anti-freeze	Water
1 litre	3 litres
2 litres	6 litres
50 ml	
200 ml	
	12 litres

5

Ginger	Water
1 spoon	5 cups
2 spoons	
5 spoons	
6 spoons	
	15 cups

An old recipe book says that to make ginger wine, we must mix 1 teaspoon of ginger essence with 5 cups of water.

Copy and complete the table.

3 THREE DIMENSIONS

LOOKING BACK

1 Name each of these shapes.

 a   **b**   **c**   **d**   **e** 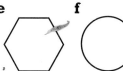   **f**

2 Name each of these solids.

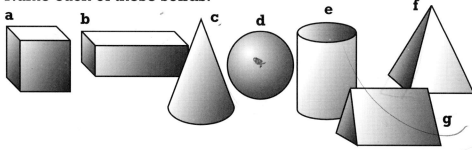

3 The objects below are based on simple solids.
For each object, name the solid.

a   **b**   **c**   **d**   **e**   **f**

     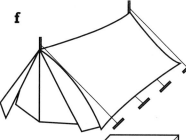

4 A dog food manufacturer chose a cuboid shape for their biscuit boxes.

    Give a few reasons why this is a good choice.

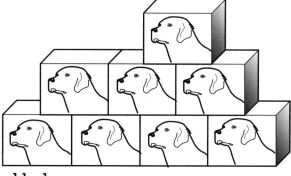

5 Three features of a cuboid are highlighted below.

a

This is a vertex.

b

This is an edge.

c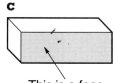

This is a face.

How many vertices does a cuboid have?

How many edges does a cuboid have?

How many faces does a cuboid have?

Isometric Drawings

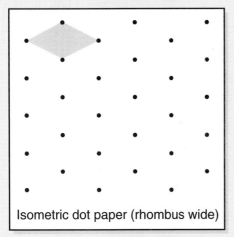

Isometric dot paper (rhombus wide)

Isometric dot paper helps you draw
3-dimensional shapes.

The shaded rhombus will help you
hold the paper the right way up.

From each point there are
6 ways to go:

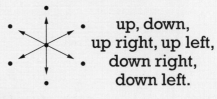

up, down,
up right, up left,
down right,
down left.

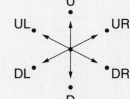

Example

Draw a $1 \times 2 \times 3$ cuboid.

Step 1 Select which way up.

Step 2 Pick a place to
start, A.

Step 3 Draw a line from A
1 unit down left
followed by a line
2 units down right.

Step 4 Draw a line from A
2 units down right
followed by a line
1 unit down left.

Step 5 Draw a line 3 units
down from each
vertex, except A.

Step 6 Complete the shape.

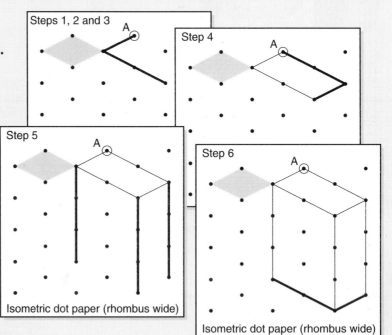

EXERCISE 1

Get Worksheet 1

You will need some isometric dot paper.

1 Worksheet 1 shows drawings of five different cuboids.
  Make copies of these drawings, starting at the points indicated.

2 Draw the following cuboids on isometric dot paper.

   a $1 \times 2 \times 4$ **b** $2 \times 1 \times 2$ **c** $3 \times 1 \times 1$ **d** $2 \times 2 \times 2$

   What name is given to cuboid **d**?

3 On isometric dot paper,

   (i)   copy each figure as shown

   (ii) complete it to make a cuboid.

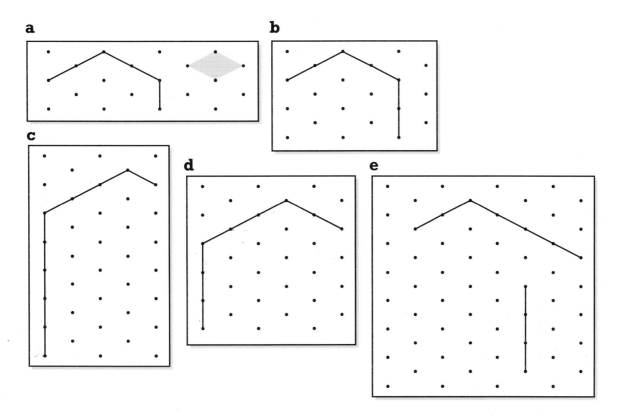

4 The following produce cuboids viewed from the bottom.

Draw them on isometric dot paper.

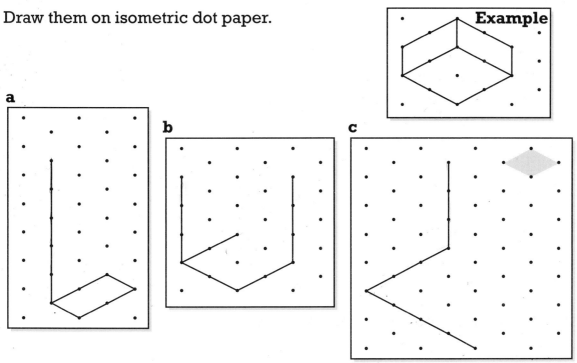

5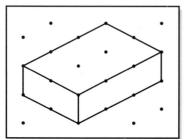

You can add dotted lines which make the cuboid appear 'see-through'.

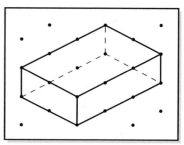

Copy the following onto isometric paper and add the dotted lines needed to make them 'see-through'.

a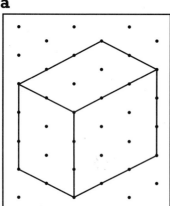

b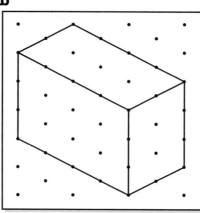

c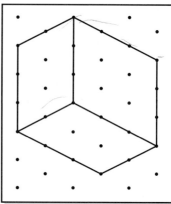

These see-through drawings are very good for looking at the properties of solids.

Labelling the vertices helps discussion.

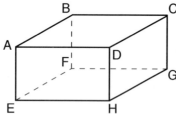

EXERCISE 2

1

The TV set is basically the cuboid ABCDEFGH.

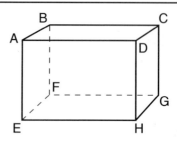

a AE is a vertical edge. Name the other three vertical edges.

b EF is a hidden edge. Name the other two hidden edges.

c E is a vertex at the bottom of the set. Name the other three.

d Name the hidden vertex.

e EFGH is a hidden face. Name the other two hidden faces.

f Name the face which represents the screen.

2  The cottage has been simplified.

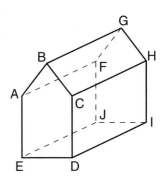

a Name the hidden vertices.

b Name the five-sided hidden face.

c CD is the nearest edge.
Name the other edges
which have the same size.

3  Compare the dice and the diagram of the cube.

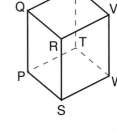

The six is represented by the face PQRS.
Opposite faces add up to seven.

a Name the face opposite PQRS.

b Name the face representing:
(i) five   (ii) two.

c What number is on the face PTWS?

4  The basic shape of a typewriter
is a triangular prism.

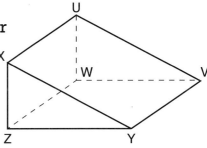

a Name the triangular faces.

b Name the sloping
rectangular face.

c Name the hidden vertex.

5 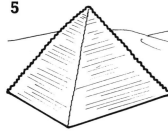 The pyramids of ancient Egypt
have square bases.

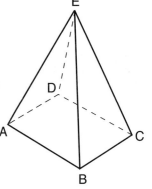

a Name the base.

b What shape is the side of a pyramid?

c Name the hidden vertex.

d Name each hidden edge.

e Name the apex (top) of the pyramid.

6 Investigate views through solids by looking at glass objects partly filled
with liquid.

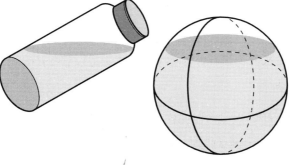

Skeleton Models

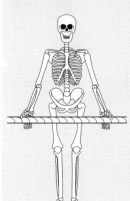

Using straws or rolled-up paper, we can make see-through models of solids. These are called **skeleton models**.

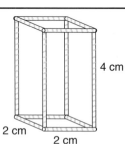

Here we have a $2 \times 3 \times 4$ skeleton cuboid.

Straws can be joined at a vertex by using small T-bars of card.

Note that the width of the T is slightly bigger than the diameter of the straw.

Planning is important.

Example

To make the above model, we need:

8 corner joins	4 straws of length 2 cm
4 straws of length 3 cm	4 straws of length 4 cm.

We need a total length of straw of 36 cm.

EXERCISE 3

1 Make a list of what you need for each skeleton model.

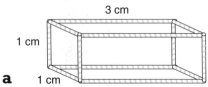

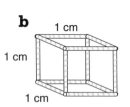

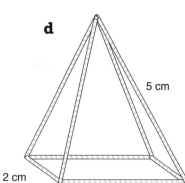

2 Maurice claimed he could make this skeleton.

Can you see what is wrong?

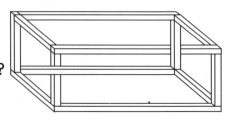

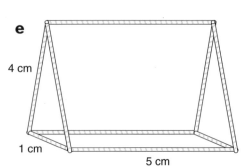

Do Worksheet 2

Nets

Reminder

This is the net of a cube since it folds up to form a cube.

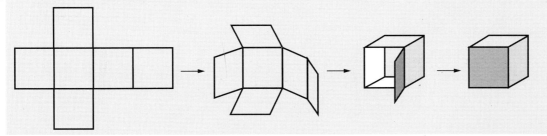

EXERCISE 4

1 Two of these are nets of cubes.

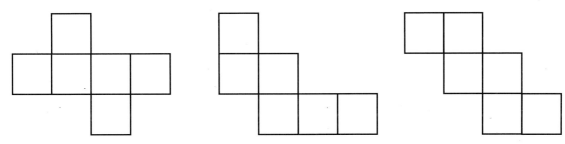

a Trace each net.

b Cut it out.

c Stick the ones which form a cube into your jotter.

Do Worksheet **3**

2 Only one of these nets makes a cuboid.

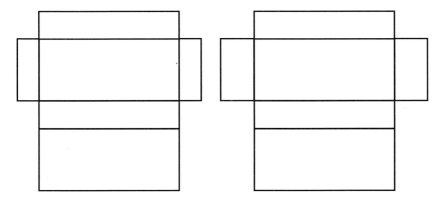

a Trace each net.

b Cut it out.

c Stick the one which forms a cuboid into your jotter.

d Suggest simple alterations to the other net to make it work.

3 The Old London Town Biscuit Company sell their biscuits in boxes with nets like this:

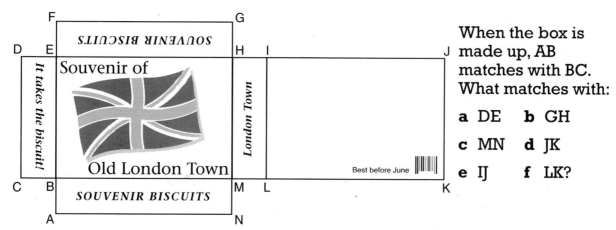

When the box is made up, AB matches with BC. What matches with:

a DE   **b** GH

c MN   **d** JK

e IJ   **f** LK?

4 The Outward Bound Company makes a tent with a sewn-in groundsheet. It is made out of three rectangles and two equilateral triangles. The net is shown below.

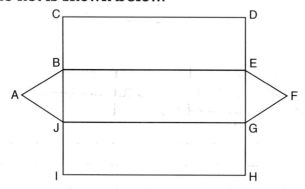

When it is sewn up, AB is stitched to BC. Where do the following stitch onto?

a AJ   **b** HG   **c** EF   **d** CD

5 A food company wants to package salt so that it is ready to use on the table. Below are two possible nets.

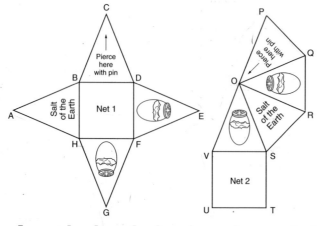

a In net 1, when the box is made up, what matches with:
  (i) AB   (ii) CD   (iii) EF   (iv) AH?

b In net 2, when the box is made up, what matches with:
  (i) OV   (ii) SR   (iii) QR   (iv) PQ?

Do Worksheet 4 5 6 7

6 Here are three cuboid boxes. Draw suitable nets on 1 cm square dot paper.

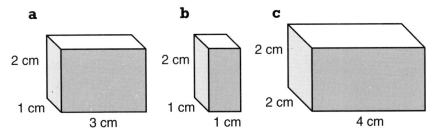

a

2 cm
1 cm
3 cm

b

2 cm
1 cm
1 cm

c

2 cm
2 cm
4 cm

Surface Area

A box manufacturer is interested in how much cardboard he is going to need. This affects the cost.

Example

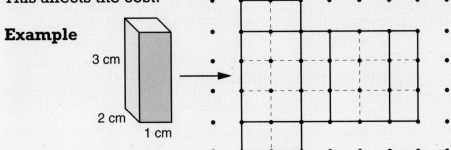

3 cm
2 cm
1 cm

When the net of the box is drawn onto 1 cm square paper, we can count that 22 square centimetres of card are needed. This is called the **surface area** of the cuboid.

EXERCISE 5

1 Work out the surface area of each of the cuboids in question 6 of Exercise 4.

2 Draw nets and work out the surface area of these cuboids.

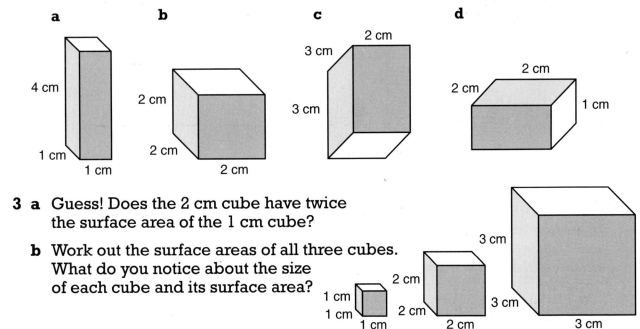

a

4 cm
1 cm
1 cm

b

2 cm
2 cm
2 cm

c

2 cm
3 cm
3 cm

d

2 cm
2 cm
1 cm

3 a Guess! Does the 2 cm cube have twice the surface area of the 1 cm cube?

b Work out the surface areas of all three cubes. What do you notice about the size of each cube and its surface area?

1 cm
1 cm
1 cm

2 cm
2 cm
2 cm

3 cm
3 cm
3 cm

CHECK-UP ON THREE DIMENSIONS

1 On isometric dot paper:

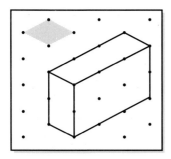
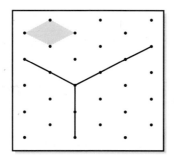
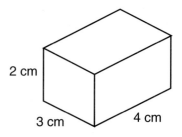

2 cm
3 cm   4 cm

a copy this drawing   **b** complete this drawing of a cuboid   **c** make this drawing.

2 An ice cube floats in water.

a Name the vertices below water.

b Name the hidden edges.

c Name four dry edges.

3 a How many corner joins do you need to make this skeleton model?

b How many straws of length 3 cm do you need?

c How many straws of length 2 cm do you need?

d What total length of straw do you need?

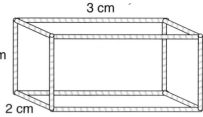

3 cm
2 cm
2 cm

4

CHESS

When the chess box is made, BC matches with CD.

What matches with:

a FG

b GH

c HI?

5 Use 1 cm square dot paper to work out the surface area of this cuboid.

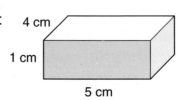

4 cm
1 cm
5 cm

4 SPENDING MONEY

LOOKING BACK

1 Write each calculator display in £ and p, like this: £5 and 10p.

   a    **b**   **c**    **d**

2 Round each sum of money to the nearest penny.

   a 28.4p   **b** 16.7p   **c** £8.3333333p   **d** £5.6666666p

3 $17\% = \frac{17}{100} = 0.17$

In the same way, write these percentages as decimals:

   a 35%   **b** 48%   **c** 83%   **d** 8%

4 Calculate: **a** 15% of £30   **b** 25% of £86   **c** 8% of £75

5 One CD costs £10.99. Melanie buys three CDs.
How much does she spend?

6 Mark is buying a pair of ice-skates.
A discount of £15 is given on the normal price.
How much does Mark pay for the skates?

7  Greg buys an old car for £150.
He fixes the engine and sells the car for £420.
Calculate Greg's profit.

8 Sophie buys an old sofa for £65. She spends £48 on material to re-cover the sofa and sells it for £110.

   a Find out if Sophie makes a profit or loss.

   b What is the profit or loss?

9 Copy and complete the plumber's bill.

⚒ INVOICE		30/1/96
A. LEEK (Plumber)		
to Mrs A. Wash, The Haven		
		£
Replace pipe		8.50
2 hours labour		17.50
Lagging		3.75
	Total £	
+ Value Added Tax (VAT)		5.21
	Total to pay £	

Shopping Bills

EXERCISE 1

1 Colin goes shopping. He buys goods costing 67p, 84p and £2.36.

   a How much does he spend?

   b Colin pays with a £10 note. How much change is he given?

2 Lisa and John go shopping for the family.

   a At the baker's they buy:

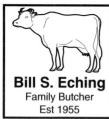

Mr Baker for your Bread

        12 rolls at 8p each
        6 strawberry tarts at 38p each
        7 jam doughnuts at 23p each
        1 chocolate gateau at £2.39.

        Calculate the amount spent at the baker's.

   b At the butcher's they buy: $\frac{1}{2}$ kg of steak mince at £6.58 per kg
        1 dozen eggs at 78p for a half dozen
        $\frac{1}{4}$ kg of bacon at £4.80 per kg.

Bill S. Eching
Family Butcher
Est 1955

        How much is spent at the butcher's?

   c At the chemist's they buy: 6 cakes of soap at 58p each
        2 tubes of toothpaste at £1.57 each
        5 toothbrushes at 79p each.

Frank E. Stein
Chemist
Est 1816

        What is the total bill at the chemist's?

   d How much do Lisa and John spend altogether?

3 From this supermarket receipt, calculate:

   a the cost of the bill

   b the change given from £10.

```
PRESCO
Thank you,
call again
03.02.97
    £
  0.12
  0.12
  0.12
  0.49
  0.63
  0.18
Total
Cash 10.00
Change
```

4 From this supermarket receipt, calculate:

   a the cost of the bill

   b the change given from £20.

```
PRESCO
Thank you,
call again
07.02.97
    £
  1.49
  0.75
  0.08
  0.08
  2.24
  3.67
Total
Cash 20.00
Change
```

Discount
Discount is money taken off the usual price.

Example 1
Usual price £30
Sale discount £6
You pay £30 − £6 = £24

Example 2
Usual price £75
Discount 20%
Discount = 20% of £75
20 ÷ 100 × 75 = £15
You pay £75 − £15 = £60

EXERCISE 2

1 A clothes shop is having a sale.

Calculate the sale price of each item.

a Jeans  £32
Discount: £5

b Skirt  £18
Discount: £4.50

c Top  £5.50
Discount: half-price

d Boots  £48
Discount: 20% off

2

		WAS	NOW
a	Child's desk	£230	£115
b	Dressing table	£497	£250
c	King-size bed	£1563	£795
d	Sofa	£1316	£675

Calculate the discount on each item of furniture.

3 Calculate the discount and the sale price of each item.

a Chess set £40 10% off

b Ladies' driver £50 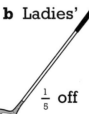 $\frac{1}{5}$ off

c Guitar £240  20% off

4 a The local cinema offers a student discount of 25%. Tommy is a student.
   (i) Calculate his discount on a ticket costing £2.60.
   (ii) How much does Tommy pay for his ticket?

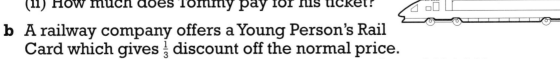

b A railway company offers a Young Person's Rail
   Card which gives $\frac{1}{3}$ discount off the normal price.
   (i) How much does a young person save on a fare of £14.82?
   (ii) How much does the young person pay?

5 This music centre usually costs £300. In a sale the shop gives a discount.

How much would the **discount** be if the price was reduced by:

a 10%   **b** 20%   **c** 25%   **d** 30%?

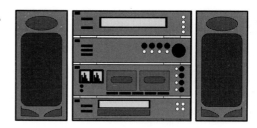

6

SUPER SALE
Spend over £50 – £5 OFF
Spend over £100 – £12 OFF
Spend over £150 – £20 OFF

ULTRA SALE
Spend over £50 - 5% OFF
Spend over £100 - 10% OFF
Spend over £150 - 15% OFF

Calculate the sale price of these items at:

a Super Sale   **b** Ultra Sale.

(i)   a pair of skates costing £65
(ii) a tracksuit costing £93
(iii) a mountain bike costing £175

7

10% off when you buy TWO of any item

How much would you pay for:
a 2 bottles of shampoo (normal price £1.85 a bottle)
b 2 tins of talcum powder (normal price £2.40 a tin)
c 2 tubes of toothpaste (normal price £1.26 a tube)?

Value Added Tax (VAT)

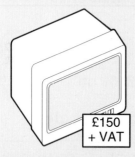

Kate hands the shop assistant £150, but it isn't enough. She has to add on 17.5% for VAT.

17.5% of £150 = $17.5 \div 100 \times 150 = £26.25$
So the TV costs £150 + £26.25 = £176.25.

The Government raises money from different taxes.
One of these is VAT.
In 1996, the rate of VAT was 17.5%.
What is the present rate of VAT?

⭐ EXERCISE 3

Take 17.5% as the rate of VAT.

1 a Calculate the VAT to be paid on the gold chain.
VAT = 17.5 ÷ 100 × 50 = £?

pure gold
£50 + VAT

Leather jacket
£180 + VAT

b Calculate the VAT
on the leather jacket.

2 Calculate the VAT to be charged on each item:

a ice skates, £60   **b** ice-hockey stick, £72

c personal stereo, £85   **d** garden shed, £280

3 a Calculate the VAT on the set of golf clubs.

b How much would you have to pay?

Champion Clubs
£120 + VAT

4

Super treads
£18.95 + VAT

Longlife battery
£32.50 + VAT

Selina's car needs a new tyre and a new battery.

a Calculate the VAT to be paid on each.

b What is Selina's total bill?

5

SUPER HOLS
Fabton Towers
7 days   £185
including VAT

Hols-Excel
Pitlochry Palace
7 days   £160
+ VAT

a Which is the cheaper
holiday?

b By how much?

6 Copy and complete these bills:

a

THE KITCHEN CUPBOARD

		£
1	soup	1.30
1	steak pie	4.80
1	apple crumble	2.30
1	coffee	0.85
	Total	
	+ VAT at 17.5%	
	To pay	

b

N. A. LEEK (Plumber)

	£
3 metres of pipe at £2.40 a metre	
4 hours labour at £12.50 an hour	
Sub-total	
+ (VAT) at 17.5%	
To pay	

c

I. B. Sparky, Electrician

	£
Plug	7.42
3 hours at £15.50 an hour	
Sub-total	
VAT at 17.5%	
To pay	

d

W. Coates (Painter)

	£
5 litres of emulsion	11.45
8 rolls of wallpaper at £6.75 per roll	
2 packets of paste at £1.45 a packet	
12 hours of labour at £11.50 an hour	
Total	
VAT at 17.5%	
To pay	

Electricity and Gas Bills

EXERCISE 4

1 Look at these meter readings.
Subtract the previous reading from the present to find the number of units used.

a

METER READING	
Present	Previous
26431	26015

b

METER READING	
Present	Previous
80423	80176

c

METER READING	
Present	Previous
07628	07054

2 Calculate the cost of these units of electricity:
   a 350 units at 8.14p per unit **b** 279 units at 7.96p per unit
   c 476 units at 9.53p per unit **d** 507 units at 7.3p per unit

3 Calculate the values of A and B in each of these:

a

METER READING	
Present	Previous
60712	60087
Number of units = A	
A units at 7.85p each	
= £B	

b

METER READING	
Present	Previous
12350	11892
Number of units = A	
A units at 7.85p each	
= £B	

Some Extra Costs
VAT is paid on electricity and gas bills. The VAT on fuel is 8%.
Customers also pay a standing charge for equipment
(even if no units are used).

4 Mrs MacFlame has been sent her electricity bill.

Sparks Electricity PLC				Meter Number
A.MacFlame, 11 High Street 11.09.96-14.12.96				131611
Meter Reading		**Charges**	**Amount (£)**	
Present	Previous			
2164	1975	A units at 7.95p	B	
		Standing Charge	7.20	
		Sub-total	C	
		VAT at 8%	D	
		TOTAL due	E	

We'll keep you plugged in

Calculate A, B, C, D and E to find how much Mrs MacFlame needs to pay.

5 Mr Watt got his electricity bill as well.

Sparks Electricity PLC				Meter Number
K. Watt, 17 High Street		14.12.96–20.03.97		131247
Meter Reading		Charges	Amount (£)	
Present	Previous			
72816	72534	*A* units at 8.21p	*B*	
		Standing Charge	7.20	
		Sub-total	*C*	We'll keep you plugged in
		VAT at 8%	*D*	
		TOTAL due	*E*	

Calculate *A, B, C, D* and *E* to find out how much Mr Watt has to pay.

6 Mrs Jewel has received her gas bill.

The Natural Gas Company		
Mrs A. Jewel, 12 Rose Road 06.04.96–10.07.96	231642	Natural Gas — your modern genie
	Amount (£)	
426 units at 20.2p per unit	*A*	
Standing charge	10.45	
Sub-total	*B*	
VAT at 8%	*C*	
TOTAL due now	*D*	

Calculate *A, B, C* and *D* to see how much she has to pay.

7 Calculate Mr Aslam's gas bill.

The Natural Gas Company		
Mr Aslam, 28 Cherry Lane 10.07.96–08.10.96	814635	Natural Gas — your modern genie
	Amount (£)	
539 units at 20.35p per unit	*A*	
Standing charge	10.45	
Sub-total	*B*	
VAT at 8%	*C*	
TOTAL due now	*D*	

Hire Purchase (HP)

Phil wants to buy the Super Zoom camera. He doesn't have £140, so he thinks about **hire purchase**.

The **deposit** has to be paid straight away. The monthly payments are called **instalments**.

SUPER ZOOM CAMERA
£140 CASH
or
HP TERMS
Deposit £20
+
6 monthly payments of £23 = £138
Total to pay = £158

What are the advantages of hire purchase?
What are the disadvantages?

EXERCISE 5

1 Jill decides to buy the computer on HP.

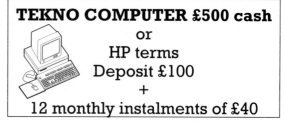

TEKNO COMPUTER £500 cash
or
HP terms
Deposit £100
+
12 monthly instalments of £40

   a How much does she pay:
(i)   as a deposit
(ii) for all 12 instalments
(iii) altogether on hire purchase?

   b How much cheaper is it to pay the cash price?

2

MOUNTAIN BIKE
£280 cash
or £50 deposit
plus 20 weekly
instalments of £13

Usman wants to buy the mountain bike.

  a What is the deposit?
  b Calculate the cost of the 20 instalments.
  c What is the total hire purchase price?
  d How much is saved by paying cash?

3

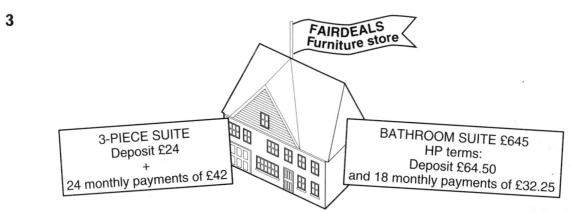

FAIRDEALS Furniture store

3-PIECE SUITE
Deposit £24
+
24 monthly payments of £42

BATHROOM SUITE £645
HP terms:
Deposit £64.50
and 18 monthly payments of £32.25

  a (i)   Calculate the cost of the 3-piece suite.
     (ii) How long is it before all the payments are made?
  b (i)   Calculate the hire purchase price of the bathroom suite.
     (ii) How much do you save by paying cash?

4 a Calculate the total hire purchase price.

   b How much cheaper is it to pay cash?

SALE OF TVs
£250 cash
or
12 monthly instalments of £25
NO DEPOSIT

5

Drive a Mercedes for less than £70 a week
1992 model: Deposit £1995
Weekly payment £69.95 (for 4 years)

How much does the car cost altogether?

6 Why is it not wise to buy too many goods on HP?

⭐ Percentage Deposit

Example

> **EXERCISE CYCLE £240**
> HP TERMS
> 25% of cash price as a deposit
> + 38 weeks at £5.50

Deposit	$= 25 \div 100 \times £240$	$= £60$
Total instalments	$= £5.50 \times 38$	$= £209$
Total HP price		$= £269$

EXERCISE 5B

1 Calculate the hire purchase price of the motorbike.

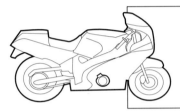

> **250 cc motorbike**
> **CASH PRICE £850**
> HP TERMS
> 10% of cash price as a deposit
> + 12 monthly payments of £68

2 The Saturday Snips
Calculate the total HP cost for each item.

a Competition kite
£40 cash or 10% deposit
+ 20 weeks at £1.80

b 3-piece graphite cue
£130 or 10% deposit + 6
weekly payments of £22

c Second-hand car £2800
or 30% of cash price + 24 monthly
payments of £99.99

d Stephen Hendry cue £50
or 10% deposit + 6 weekly
payments of £8

e Walking boots £45
or 10% of cash price
+ 20 weeks at £2.20

f Sports bag £27
or 15% of cash price + 20
weekly payments of £1.25

g Food processor
£54 or 20% of
cash price + 10
weekly payments
of £4.80

Profit and Loss

Example

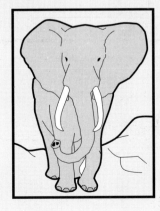

A shop bought some wildlife posters
for £1.50 each.

It sold them for £2.00 each.

It made a profit of
£2.00 − £1.50 = £0.50
on each poster.

EXERCISE 6

1 A shop bought model rhinos for £3.00 each.
It sold them for £2.00 each.
It made a loss.

How much money did the shop lose on each rhino?

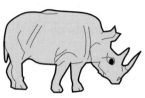

2 Tom and Sara run an antiques shop.
The buying and selling prices of some items are shown below.

Work out the profit or loss on each item.

Clock
Bought for £87
Sold for £105

Model steam engine
Bought for £50
Sold for £38

Paper weight
Bought for £38
Sold for £35

Lamp
Bought for £17
Sold for £15

Necklace
Bought for £12
Sold for £40

Writing desk
Bought for £62
Sold for £145

Candle holder
Bought for £3
Sold for £14

Jug
Bought for £25
Sold for £37

3 Dave estimates that it costs him 48p to make a
jar of marmalade.
He sells it for 72p a jar.

a Calculate his profit on one jar of marmalade.
b What is his profit on 100 jars?

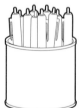

4 A shopkeeper buys pens at 17p each.
He sells them at 26p each.

a Calculate his profit on one pen.
b What is his profit on 50 pens?

5 Judy makes soft toys. It costs her £1.84 to make each toy.
She sells them for £6 each.

a Calculate the profit Judy makes on each soft toy.
b Judy gives her profit to charity.
How much can she give to charity if she sells 20 soft toys?

6  Wendy bought an old car for £185.
She spent £78 on new parts for the car.
She sold the car for £250.
Calculate her profit or loss.

CHECK-UP ON SPENDING MONEY

1

GARDEN HUTS		
SUPER DISCOUNTS		
	WAS	NOW
8 feet × 6 feet	£290	£255

Calculate the discount on the hut.

2 A discount of 20% is given at a sale.

Watches £50

  a What is the discount on the watch?
  b How much do you have to pay for the watch?

3

GO-KARTS FOR SALE
£640 + VAT (at 17.5%)

  a Calculate the VAT on a go-kart.
  b How much would you pay altogether for the go-kart?

4 How many units have been used?

METER READING	
Present	Previous
37254	36980

5 Calculate *A, B, C, D* and *E* to
find out how much Mrs Spark
has to pay for her electricity.

Sure-Glow Electricity PLC				Meter Number
A. Spark, 11 Orange Flame 12.07.96–14.10.96				274316

Meter Reading		Charges	Amount (£)	
Present	Previous			
27536	27148	*A* units at 8.02p	*B*	*The shining service*
		Standing Charge	9.43	
		Sub-total	*C*	
		VAT at 8%	*D*	
		TOTAL due	*E*	

6

TRACKSUIT
£99.99 cash
or
HP TERMS
Deposit £25
+ 20 weeks at £4.20

  a Calculate the total hire purchase price.
  b How much cheaper is it to pay cash for
     the tracksuit?

7

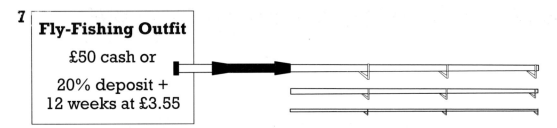

Fly-Fishing Outfit

£50 cash or

20% deposit +
12 weeks at £3.55

    a Calculate the deposit.
    b Calculate the total amount of the weekly payments.
    c What is the total hire purchase price?

8 Melanie restores furniture.
    She buys an old rocking chair for £18.
    She spends £38 repairing and painting it.
    She sells the chair for £75.

    Calculate Melanie's profit.

Weight

Reminder | Weight is measured in **grams**, **kilograms** and **tonnes**.

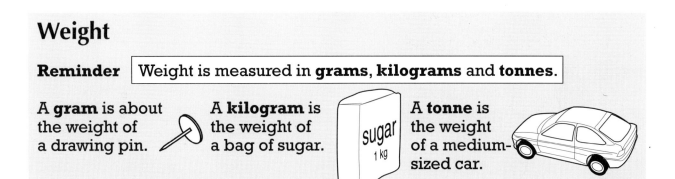

A **gram** is about the weight of a drawing pin.

A **kilogram** is the weight of a bag of sugar.

sugar 1 kg

A **tonne** is the weight of a medium-sized car.

LOOKING BACK AT WEIGHT

Which unit of weight would you use to measure the following?

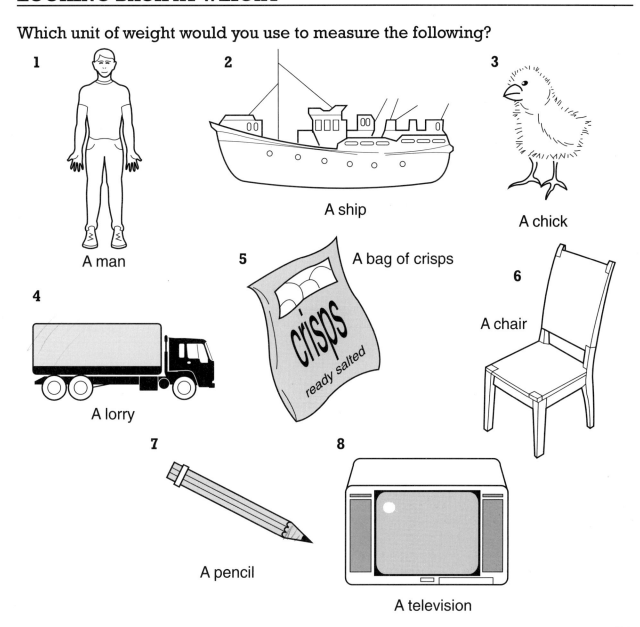

1 A man

2 A ship

3 A chick

4 A lorry

5 A bag of crisps

6 A chair

7 A pencil

8 A television

Scales

We use different types of scales to measure weight. The items on these scales all weigh 500 grams.

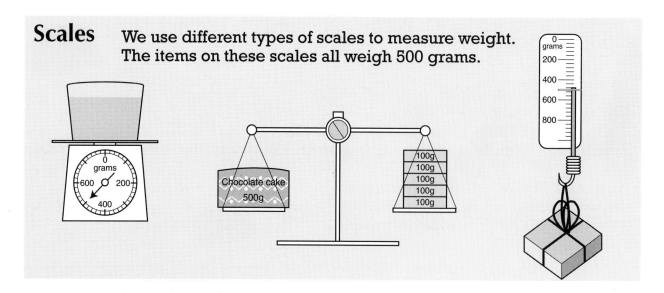

EXERCISE 1

Write down the weights of the items on these scales.

Kilograms and Grams

1 kilogram = 1000 grams

These scales measure kilograms (kg) and grams (g).

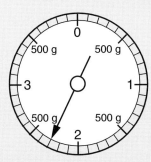

Each kilogram is divided
into 10 small steps.
1000 g ÷ 10 = 100 g
Each small step is worth 100 g.

This arrow is pointing to **2 kg 300 g**.

Each kilogram is divided
into 4 small steps.
1000 g ÷ 4 = 250 g
Each small step is worth 250 g.

This arrow is pointing to **1 kg 750 g**.

Remember to check what each small step is worth.

EXERCISE 2

Write down the weights, in kilograms and grams, shown on these scales.

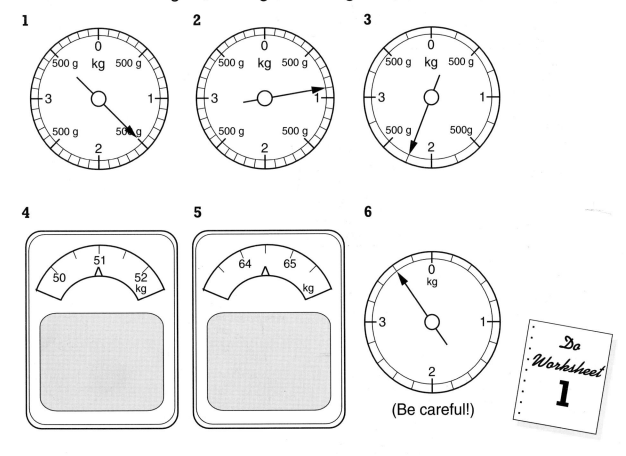

1

2

3

4

5

6

(Be careful!)

Do Worksheet **1**

Changing

kilograms ──── × 1000 ── grams

grams ──── ÷ 1000 ── kilograms

Examples

1 3 kg = 3 × 1000 = 3000 g
2 7 kg 500 g = 7 × 1000 + 500 = 7500 g
3 2000 g = 2000 ÷ 1000 = 2 kg
4 9400 g = 9000 ÷ 1000 + 400 = 9 kg 400 g
5 6200 g = 6200 ÷ 1000 = 6.2 kg
6 5.3 kg = 5.3 × 1000 = 5300 g

EXERCISE 3

1 Change these weights into grams.

  a 4 kg   **b** 9 kg   **c** 14 kg   **d** 2 kg 500 g   **e** 6 kg 850 g

  f 1 kg 420 g   **g** 9 kg 100 g   **h** 2 kg 950 g   **i** 3 kg 50 g   **j** 4 kg 95 g

2 Change these weights to kilograms and grams.

  a 8000 g   **b** 5000 g   **c** 18 000 g   **d** 4200 g

  e 6150 g   **f** 3030 g   **g** 2004 g   **h** 980 g

3 Change these weights into kilograms (by dividing by 1000).
For example: 5200 g ÷ 1000 = 5.2 kg.

  a 3100 g   **b** 9150 g   **c** 11 000 g   **d** 10 060 g   **e** 1900 g

  f 160 g   **g** 32 g   **h** 540 g   **i** 7234 g   **j** 6 g

4 Change these weights into grams (by multiplying by 1000).

  a 1.4 kg   **b** 18.2 kg   **c** 3.268 kg   **d** 1.65 kg

  e 0.9 kg   **f** 0.25 kg   **g** 0.003 kg

5 Change these weights into grams (by multiplying the kilograms by 1000, then adding on the grams).

  a 2 kg 500 g   **b** 3 kg 250 g   **c** 7 kg 850 g   **d** 12 kg 100 g   **e** 4 kg 420 g

  f 6 kg 40 g   **g** 4 kg 50 g   **h** 1 kg 25 g   **i** 5 kg 36 g   **j** 1 kg 4 g

Using Weight

EXERCISE 4

1 Here is part of a recipe for cherry cake.

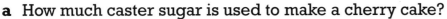

Cherry cake	
150 g caster sugar	200 g flour
150 g butter or margarine	pinch of salt
3 eggs	150 g cherries

   a How much caster sugar is used to make a cherry cake?
   b What weight of cherries would you need for two cherry cakes?
   c Kyle has a dozen eggs. How many cherry cakes can he make with them?
   d Lorna buys a 1 kg bag of flour. She makes a cherry cake.
     How much flour has she left?
   e Sara wants to make a cherry cake. She has only 73 g of butter.
     How much margarine will she need to put in to make her cake?

2 Here is what is in Mrs Currie's shopping basket.

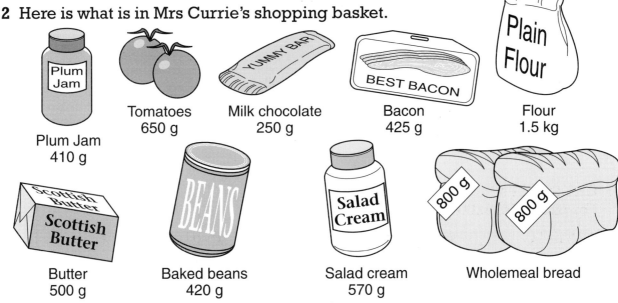

Plum Jam 410 g
Tomatoes 650 g
Milk chocolate 250 g
Bacon 425 g
Flour 1.5 kg
Butter 500 g
Baked beans 420 g
Salad cream 570 g
Wholemeal bread

   a How many grams of flour did she buy?
   b How much heavier than the plum jam is the salad cream?
   c What is the total weight of the bread in kilograms?
   d What is the lightest item she bought?
   e What is the total weight of Mrs Currie's shopping?

3 A book weighs 480 grams. Six of the books are parcelled
   up to be sent through the post. The packaging and
   wrapping paper weigh 240 grams.
   a What is the total weight of the parcel?   b Write this weight in kilograms.

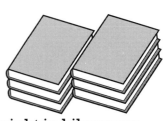

4 A bowl with flour in it weighs 1 kg 260 g. The bowl weighs 835 grams.
   How heavy is the flour?

Area

The area of a shape is how much surface it covers.

Area is measured in square units.

square millimetres

Each square in the portcullis is about 1 sq. mm.

square centimetres

Each fingernail is about 1 sq. cm.

square metres

A bedspread is about 2 sq. m.

square kilometres

Ireland is about 84 000 sq. km.

Counting Squares

Each square is a square centimetre.
The shaded rectangle covers 12 squares.
We say the rectangle has an area of
12 square centimetres.
We write: **area of rectangle = 12 cm²**.

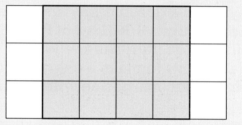

LOOKING BACK ON AREA

---

1 Find the area of each shape by counting the squares.
Write your answer like this: Area = ... cm².

a

b

c

d

e

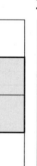

f

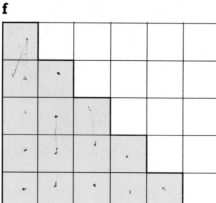

g

2 You will need a 1 cm square acetate grid. Place the grid over these shapes.
Count the squares to find the area of each shape.

a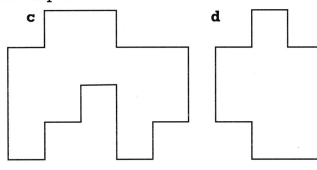

b

c

d

e

Parts of a Square

Some shapes do not cover complete squares.
This shape covers **10 whole squares** and **2 half squares**.
The 2 half squares make 1 whole square.
Area of shape = 11 cm².

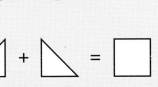

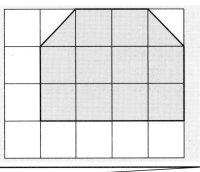

EXERCISE 5

Remember: 2 halves make 1 whole.

Count the squares in each of these shapes.
Count each part of a square as a half.

1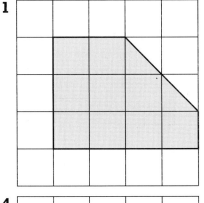

2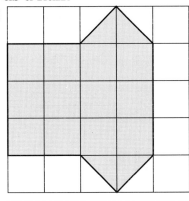

3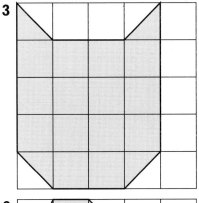

4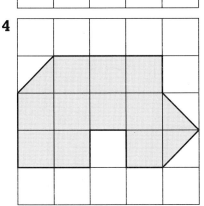

5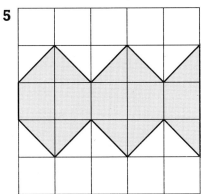

6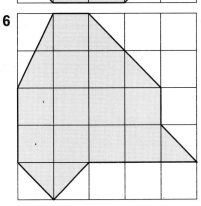

Area of Irregular Shapes

When a shape does not have straight edges, you can't get an exact area by counting squares. To get a good idea of the area:

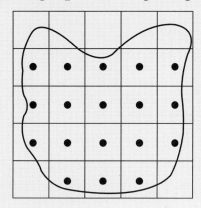

count the whole squares
count parts that are half or more than a half as squares
don't count parts that are less than a half.

This shape has an area of about 18 square centimetres or 18 cm².

Do Worksheet **2**

EXERCISE 6

These are maps of islands.
Each square on the map stands for 1 square kilometre.

Palm Island has an area of about 16 square kilometres.

We can write this as 16 km².

Palm Island

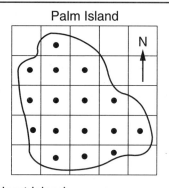

Coral Island

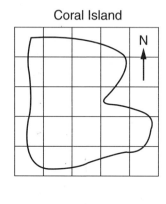

Isle of Bays

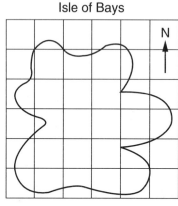

Heart Island

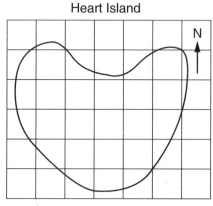

1 Write the areas of the other three islands in square kilometres (km²).

2 Which of the three islands has the largest area?

3 How much bigger than Coral Island is Heart Island?

4 This is Dolphin Island.
   a To which island does it look closest in area?
   b Estimate the area of Dolphin Island in square kilometres.
   c Count the squares to find the area of Dolphin Island.

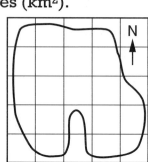

Calculating Area

Area of a rectangle = length × breadth

Area = *l* × *b*

Length 5 cm

Breadth 4 cm

Example 1 How many squares make up this rectangle?

Four rows of five
= 4 × 5 = 20 squares
Area = 20 square centimetres or 20 cm².

Example 2 Calculate the area of this rectangle.

6 cm

3 cm

Area of rectangle = length × breadth
= 6 cm × 3 cm
= 18 cm².

(Note: you can't use a grid because the rectangle is not drawn accurately.)

EXERCISE 7

Do Worksheet 3

1 Bashir collects stamps. These are his four favourite stamps.

a 4 cm 3 cm

b 2 cm 2 cm

c 5 cm 3 cm

d 4 cm 4.5 cm

Calculate the area of each stamp.

2 Gianna has six posters on her wall. Calculate the area of each poster.

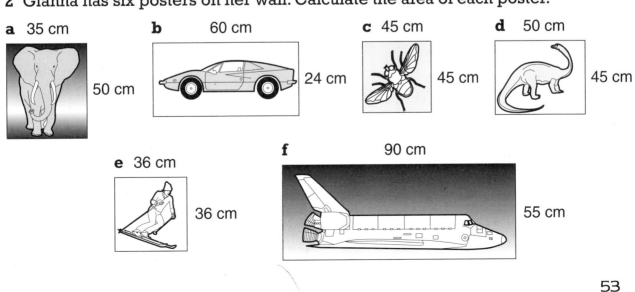

a 35 cm 50 cm

b 60 cm 24 cm

c 45 cm 45 cm

d 50 cm 45 cm

e 36 cm 36 cm

f 90 cm 55 cm

3 Calculate the area of the front of the LP record, the compact disc, the video tape and the cassette tape.

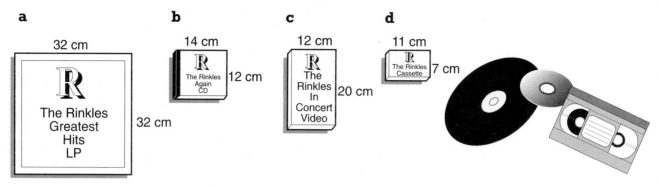

a 32 cm 32 cm The Rinkles Greatest Hits LP

b 14 cm 12 cm The Rinkles Again CD

c 12 cm 20 cm The Rinkles In Concert Video

d 11 cm 7 cm The Rinkles Cassette

4 This is a plan of Bijal's garden.
(The sizes are in metres, so the areas will be in square metres.)

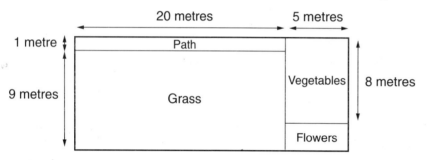

20 metres | 5 metres
1 metre — Path
9 metres — Grass
Vegetables | 8 metres
Flowers

a Calculate the area of:
   (i) the path   (ii) the grass   (iii) the vegetable patch.
b (i) How long is the whole garden?
   (ii) How broad is the whole garden?
   (iii) Calculate the area of the whole garden.
c (i) How long and how broad is the flower bed?
   (ii) Calculate the area of the flower bed.

5 Which has the larger area, a rectangle measuring 8 cm by 5 cm or a square that measures 6 cm by 6 cm?

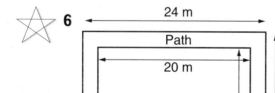

6 24 m
Path
20 m
Grass   16 m
20 m
Path

This is a plan of Emma's garden.
a Calculate the area of the whole garden.
b Calculate the area of the grass.
c Subtract the area of the grass from the total area to find the area of the path.

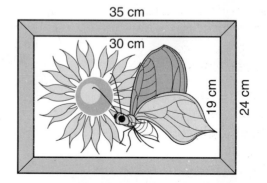

35 cm
30 cm
19 cm
24 cm

7 This is a picture in its frame.
The frame is shaded.
Calculate the shaded area.
(Follow the steps in question 6.)

Area of a Triangle

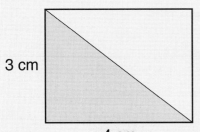

3 cm

4 cm

Area of the rectangle = $l \times b$
= 4 cm $\times$ 3 cm
= 12 cm².
Area of the shaded triangle
= half the area of the rectangle
= 12 cm² ÷ 2 = 6 cm².

| **Area of a triangle = half the area of the rectangle** |

Do Worksheet **4**

EXERCISE 8

1 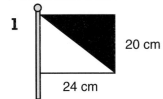 This flag measures 24 cm by 20 cm.

20 cm

24 cm

a Calculate the area of the rectangle.
b Calculate the area of the shaded triangle.

2 The front of a box of Luxury Chocolates is in the shape of a right-angled triangle.
Calculate the area of the front of the box.

12 cm

Luxury Chocolates

16 cm

3 (i)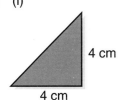

4 cm

4 cm

(ii) 2 cm

4 cm

(iii) 3 cm

3 cm

(iv) 3 cm

5 cm

(v)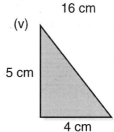

5 cm

4 cm

Sam has a set of wooden tiles.
There are rectangles, squares and right-angled triangles.

a Calculate the area of each of the tiles.
b Which tile has the greatest area?

4 Angela's field is a rectangle 40 metres by 28 metres.
She puts up a diagonal fence to separate the horse and the sheep.
What area of the field does the horse get?

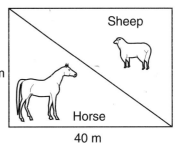

Sheep

28 m

Horse

40 m

5 Tessa makes stained glass windows out of pieces of coloured glass.

Calculate the area of each of the coloured pieces of glass.

a 6 cm

Yellow

8 cm

b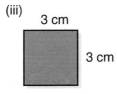

2 cm

Green

2 cm

c 5 cm

Red

1 cm

d 5 cm

Blue

3 cm

Volume

Reminder The volume of an object is how much space it takes up.
A rugby ball has a larger volume that a golf ball.
Volume is measured in cubic units.

cubic millimetres (mm³)   cubic centimetres (cm³)   cubic metres (m³)

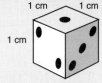

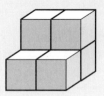

A grain of salt is about
1 cubic millimetre.

A dice is roughly
1 cubic centimetre.

A bed takes up the space
of about 1 cubic metre.

Counting Cubes

This shape is made up of 6 cubes.
Each cube represents 1 cubic centimetre.
We say the volume of the shape is **6 cubic centimetres**.
We write: **volume of shape = 6 cm³**.

LOOKING BACK ON VOLUME

Count the cubes in each shape to find the volume of the shape.
Write your answer like this: Volume of A = ... cm³.

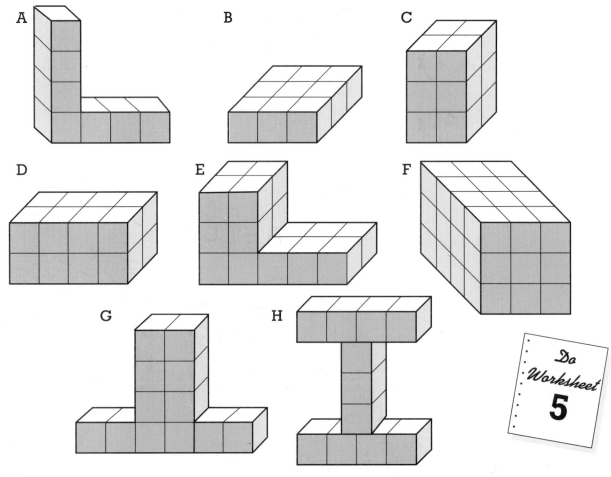

Do
Worksheet
5

Layers

This solid is made up of 2 identical layers of centimetre cubes.

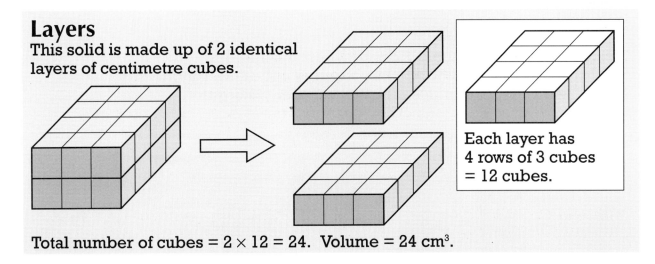

Each layer has 4 rows of 3 cubes = 12 cubes.

Total number of cubes = 2 × 12 = 24. Volume = 24 cm³.

EXERCISE 9

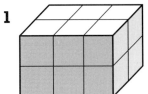

1   **a** Write down how many cubes are in each layer.
   b How many layers are there?
   c Multiply to find the volume of the cuboid in cubic centimetres (cm³).

Follow the instructions in question **1** to find the volume of each of these cuboids.

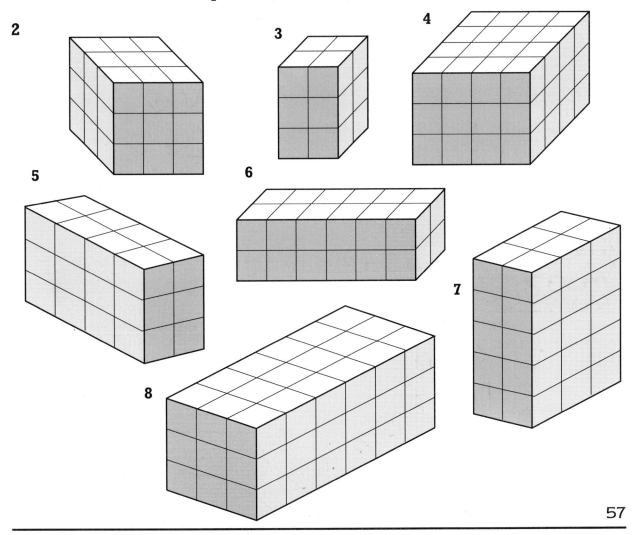

Calculating Volume

This picture shows a cuboid 3 cm by 2 cm by 2 cm.
To find the volume without counting cubes, we use the formula:

volume of cuboid = length × breadth × height
$$= 3 \text{ cm} \times 2 \text{ cm} \times 2 \text{ cm}$$
$$= 12 \text{ cm}^3$$

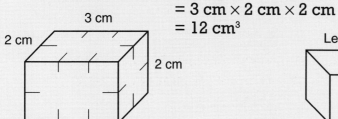

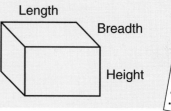

Length
Breadth
Height

Do Worksheet **6**

EXERCISE 10

1 A box of chocolates is 16 cm by 12 cm by 5 cm.

Use the formula to calculate the volume of the box of chocolates.

2  A double compact disc case is 14 cm by 12 cm by 1 cm thick.

Calculate the volume of the compact disc case.

3 The plastic case for a video is 20 cm by 10 cm by 2.5 cm.

Calculate the volume of the video case.

When the length, breadth and height are in metres, the volume is in cubic metres.

4 A blanket box is 2 metres by 2 metres by 1 metre.
Calculate the volume of the blanket box in cubic metres.

5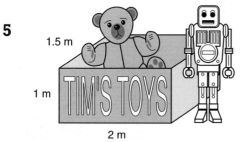
1.5 m
1 m
2 m

A toy box is in the shape of a cuboid.
It is 2 metres by 1.5 metres by 1 metre.

Calculate the volume of the toy box.

6 Here are the sizes of some rooms in a school.

Work out the volume of each room in cubic metres.

a Science Lab

3 metres
6 metres
15 metres

b Maths Room

3 m
5 m
11 m

c Medical Room

3 m
3 m
8 m

7

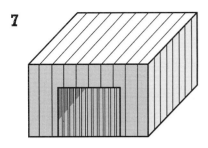

A rabbit hutch is in the shape of a cuboid.
It is 3 metres by 2 metres by 1.5 metres.

Calculate the volume of the hutch.

8 Ronald wants to buy an oil tank. He wants the one that holds more oil.
Which one should he choose, A or B? (Show all your working.)

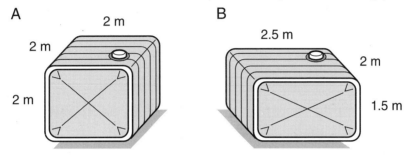

**When the length, breadth and height are in millimetres,
the volume is in cubic millimetres.**

9 Calculate the volume of each of these objects in cubic millimetres.

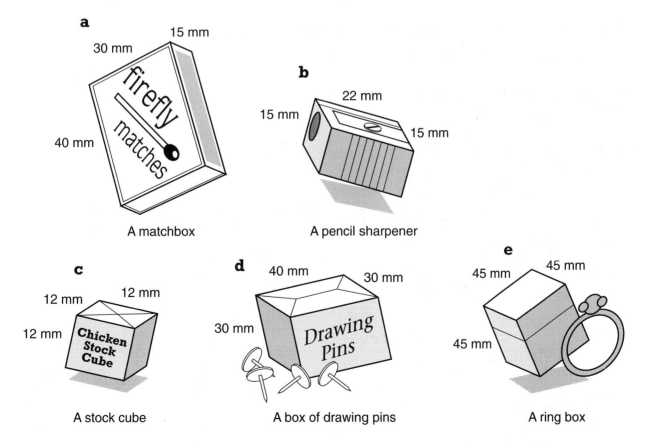

a
15 mm
30 mm
40 mm
A matchbox

b
22 mm
15 mm
15 mm
A pencil sharpener

c
12 mm
12 mm
12 mm
A stock cube

d
40 mm
30 mm
30 mm
A box of drawing pins

e
45 mm
45 mm
45 mm
A ring box

Volume of Liquids

The volume of a liquid is usually measured in litres.

1000 cubic centimetres = 1 litre (l)

A cubic centimetre is usually called a **millilitre (ml)**.

On this jug, each litre is divided into 5 small divisions.
1 litre ÷ 5
= 1000 ml ÷ 5 = 200 ml
Each small division is worth 200 ml.
This jug contains 800 ml of liquid.

EXERCISE 11

1 Write down the volume of liquid, in millilitres, in each of these jugs.

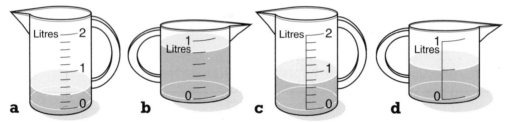

a   **b**   **c**   **d**

2 Write down the volume of liquid, in litres and millilitres, in each of these jugs.

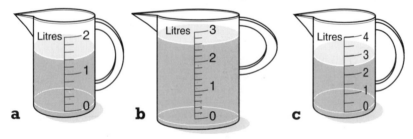

a   **b**   **c**

3 There is 1 litre of cola in this bottle.
  a How many millilitres is this?
  b Rebecca drinks 200 ml of the cola. Peter drinks 150 ml of it.
     How many millilitres of cola are left?

4 Kalil buys a large bottle of orange juice for a party.
It holds 3 litres of juice. Each glass holds 150 ml of juice.
How many glasses can Kalil fill from the bottle of orange juice?

5 The instructions on Gail's bottle of cough medicine read:
'Two 5 ml spoonfuls three times a day'.
  a How many millilitres of cough medicine should she take at a time?
  b How many millilitres would she take in a day?
  c The bottle holds 300 ml of cough syrup.
     For how many days will her medicine last?

6 A small carton of apple juice contains 200 ml of juice.
A case of juice holds 40 of the small cartons.

   a Calculate how much apple juice is in the large case.
   b Write this volume in litres.

7 Karen has a party. Her friends all bring something to drink to the party.
This is what they brought.

   a Which kind of drink is there the most of?
   b How many millilitres of ginger beer are there?
   c How much do they have to drink altogether?
      Give your answer in litres and millilitres.
   d We can write 500 ml of cola as 0.5 litre.
      Write 750 ml of apple juice in this way.

CHECK-UP ON WEIGHT, AREA AND VOLUME

Weight

1 Write down the weight shown on each of these scales.

a 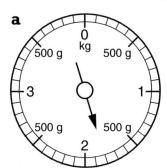   **b**   **c**

2 A bag of flour holds 1.5 kg.
Andy uses 650 g to make some cakes.

How much flour is left?

3 Put these weights in order, with the lightest first.

0.85 kg   800 g   0.805 kg

Area

4 a Write down a good estimate for the area of the shaded shape.

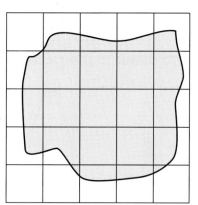

b Find the area of this shaded shape.

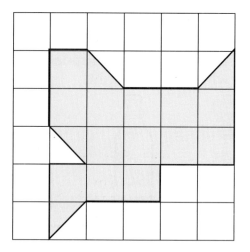

5 Calculate the areas of these shapes.
Remember to give the units in your answers.

a

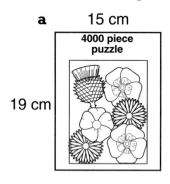

15 cm

4000 piece puzzle

19 cm

b

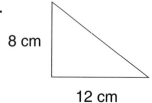

23 mm

USA

23 mm

10c

c

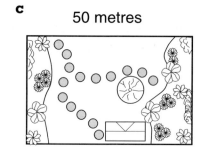

50 metres

31 metres

6 Calculate the area of this triangle.

8 cm

12 cm

Volume

7 Count the cubes to find the volume of this solid in cubic centimetres.

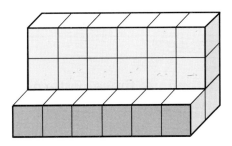

8 Calculate the volume of this block of cheese.

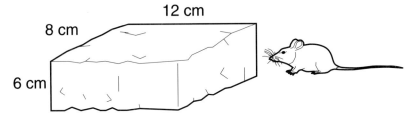

9 How many 200 ml glasses can be filled from a 2 litre bottle of cola?

LOOKING BACK

1 Copy and continue these patterns.

a

      1   2   3   **?**   **?**
                                                4   5

b

      1   2   3   **?**   **?**
                                                4   5

2 Copy and continue these 'adding on' patterns.

a | + 2 > 2, 4, 6, 8, 10, ... , ... , ... , ...

b | + 5 > 5, 10, 15, 20, 25, ... , ... , ... , ...

c | + 3 > 4, 7, 10, 13, 16, ... , ... , ... , ...

3 Write down the missing numbers on each card.

a

+ 11 >

6 ——▶ 17
12 ——▶ ?
3 ——▶ ?
15 ——▶ ?

b

− 4 >

7 ——▶ 3
11 ——▶ ?
15 ——▶ ?
23 ——▶ ?

c

× 2 >

10 ——▶ 20
13 ——▶ ?
9 ——▶ ?
18 ——▶ ?

4 Copy and complete the table.

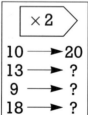

1 star   2 stars   3 stars   4 stars
5 points   10 points   15 points   ? points

Number of stars	1	2	3	4	5	6	7
Number of points	5	10					

Patterns

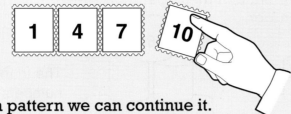

When we spot a pattern we can continue it.

Example

The numbers 1, 4, 7, 10 form a simple pattern.
Can you continue the pattern?

Check that you get the next number by adding 3 to the previous one.

previous number —— $+ 3$ —— **next number**

Knowing this rule, you can continue the pattern: 1, 4, 7, 10, **13**, **16**, **19**, ...

EXERCISE 1

1 For each pattern below: (i) find a rule   (ii) continue the pattern.

  a 1, 3, 5, 7, 9, ... , ...   **e** 36, 42, 48, 54, 60, ... , ...

  b 1, 8, 15, 22, 29, ... , ...   **f** 26, 36, 46, 56, 66, ... , ...

  c 105, 104, 103, 102, 101, ... , ...   **g** 22, 33, 44, 55, 66, ... , ...

  d 98, 93, 88, 83, 78, ... , ...   **h** 2, 4, 8, 16, 32, ... , ...

2 Draw the next picture for each of these patterns.

  a

  b

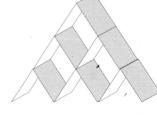

3 Draw the next picture for each of these patterns.
Write down the next number.

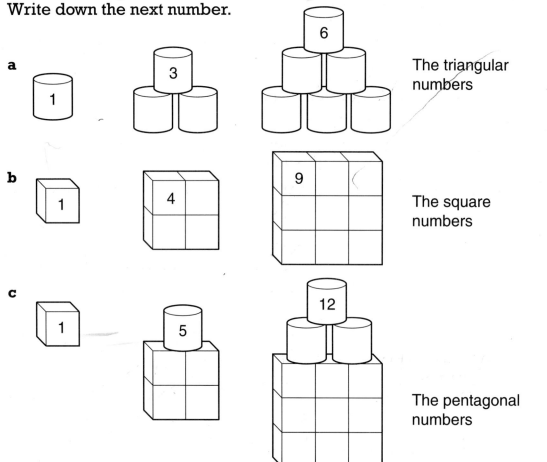

a

1

3

6

The triangular numbers

b

1

4

9

The square numbers

c

1

5

12

The pentagonal numbers

4 This pattern was invented around 1000 BC in China.
Each part of the pattern stands for a number.
Some numbers are made with black dots and some with white.

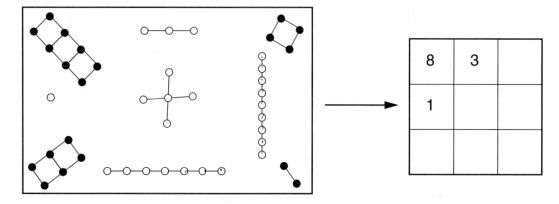

8	3	
1		

a Copy and complete the square on the right. (Think of the dots.)
b What colour are the even numbers?
c What colour are the odd numbers?
d Where in the square do you find even numbers?
e Add each row. What do you notice?
f Add each column. What do you notice?

Describing Number Patterns

This well known pattern is called the **counting numbers**.

| 1 | 2 | 3 | 4 | 5 | 6 | 7 | 8 | 9 | 10 | ... |

We can make new patterns by using a rule to change the counting numbers.

Example

Rule

Birds	**Counting numbers**	1	2	3	4	5	6	7	8	9	10
	Rule					times 2					
Legs	**New pattern**	2	4	6	8	10	12	14	16	18	20

×2

Get Worksheet **1**

EXERCISE 2

1 Use the rules to make new patterns.

a

Counting numbers	1	2	3	4	5	6	7	8	9	10
Rule					times 9					
New pattern	9	18								

Rule ×9

b

Counting numbers	1	2	3	4	5	6	7	8	9	10
Rule					times 10					
New pattern	10	20								

Rule ×10

2 Here you will find that the patterns are made by counting legs.

a

horses	1	2	3	4	5	6	7	8	9	10
Rule					times 4					
legs	4	8								

Rule ×4

b

bees	1	2	3	4	5	6	7	8	9	10
Rule					times 6					
legs	6	12								

Rule ×6

c

starfish	1	2	3	4	5	6	7	8	9	10
Rule					times 5					
legs	5	10								

Rule ×5

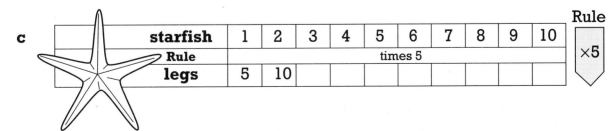

3 The rules don't need to be **times**.
Try these.

a

Counting numbers	1	2	3	4	5	6	7	8	9	10	+9
New pattern	10	11	12								

b

Counting numbers	1	2	3	4	5	6	7	8	9	10	+7
New pattern	8	9	10								

c

Counting numbers	1	2	3	4	5	6	7	8	9	10	+20
New pattern	21	22									

4 a Making tea?
Rule: use one spoon per person and one for the pot.

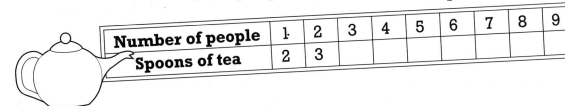

Number of people	1	2	3	4	5	6	7	8	9	10	+1
Spoons of tea	2	3									

Copy and complete the table to show the pattern.

b Three teachers take pupils on a bus journey.
Rule: the number of seats needed is 3 more than the number of pupils.

Number of pupils	1	2	3	4		10	+3
Number of seats	4						

Copy and complete the table.

c At the Theme Park.
Rule: it costs £5 to get in and £1 per ride.

+5

Number of rides	1	2	3	4	5	6
Total cost (£)	6					

Make a table that shows the pattern of costs as the number of rides goes from 1 to 10.

d The number of spaces between lamp-posts is one less than the number of lamp-posts.

−1

Make a table that shows the pattern of spaces as the number of posts goes from 1 to 10.

Sometimes a rule for a pattern has two steps.

Example

Counting numbers	1	2	3	4	5	6	7	8	9	10	×3
After step 1	3	6	9	12	15	18	21	24	27	30	
After step 2	4	7	10	13	16	19	22	25	28	31	+1

Counting numbers —⟨ × 3 ⟩——⟨ + 1 ⟩— New pattern

4, 7, 10, 13, 16, 19, 22, 25, 28, 31

Get Worksheet 2

EXERCISE 2B

1 Use the numbers 1 to 10 and the rules below to make new number patterns.

   a Counting numbers —⟨ × 2 ⟩——⟨ + 1 ⟩— New pattern

   b Counting numbers —⟨ × 2 ⟩——⟨ + 2 ⟩— New pattern

   c Counting numbers —⟨ × 5 ⟩——⟨ + 1 ⟩— New pattern

   d Counting numbers —⟨ × 3 ⟩——⟨ − 1 ⟩— New pattern

   e Counting numbers —⟨ × 7 ⟩——⟨ − 1 ⟩— New pattern

   f Counting numbers —⟨ × 9 ⟩——⟨ + 2 ⟩— New pattern

2 The bank will change £1 coins into 10p coins and keep 10p for the trouble!

One pound coins —⟨ × 10 ⟩——⟨ − 1 ⟩— 10p coins

Complete the table to find the final pattern: 9, 19, 29, ...

One pound coins	1	2	3	4	5	6	7	8	9	10	×10
After step 1	10	20	30								
Number of 10p coins	9	19	29								−1

3 Bryan's train set has an engine with 6 wheels
and carriages with 4 wheels.

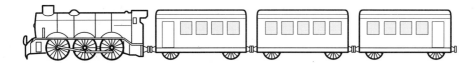

a Check that the number of wheels on a train is:
four times the number of parts of the train and add two.

Parts ——— ×4 —— +2 —— Wheels

b Make a table to show the pattern of wheels as the number of parts goes up
from 1 to 10.

4 The cost of a call is 10p for the connection and 5p for each minute.

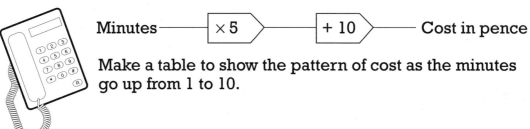

Minutes ——— ×5 —— +10 —— Cost in pence

Make a table to show the pattern of cost as the minutes
go up from 1 to 10.

5 The cost of buying tickets for the theatre is £8 for each ticket
and a £3 booking fee.

Number of tickets ——— ×8 —— +3 —— Cost in pounds

THE
NEWTOWN
PLAYERS
present
**The last
tango in
Tonbridge**
Family comedy
From Tuesday
18th June

Show the number pattern of costs by looking at party sizes
growing from just 1 person to 10 people.

6 Number in party ——— ×4 —— −2 —— Total cost in pounds

Triassic Park
£4 each
£2 deposit will be
returned per party.

Show the number pattern of costs for
parties of size 1 to 10.

7 Jack knows that he needs to cook a joint for 20 minutes per kilogram plus
30 minutes.

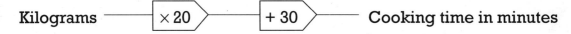

Kilograms ——— ×20 —— +30 —— Cooking time in minutes

Work out the number pattern of cooking times by considering joints with
weights from 1 kg to 10 kg.

Spotting the Rule

Look at this pattern: **3 5 7 9 11 ...**   The numbers go up in **twos.**

This suggests the rule ⟩ × 2 ⟩

... but this would give: **2 4 6 8 10 ...**

We need to **add one** to each of these to get our pattern.

So the rule is: — ⟩ × 2 ⟩ —— ⟩ + 1 ⟩ —

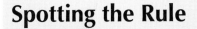

Check it out!

Counting numbers	1	2	3	4	5	6	7	8	9	10
Pattern	3	5	7	9	11	13	15	17	19	21

EXERCISE 3

1 Each of the following has been made by changing the counting numbers using a simple rule like:

⟩ × a number ⟩

Find the rule for each.

a 5 10 15 20 25 30 35 40 45 50   **b** 10 20 30 40 50 60 70 80 90 100
c 6 12 18 24 30 36 42 48 54 60   **d** 4   8 12 16 20 24 28 32 36   40
e 9 18 27 36 45 54 63 72 81 90   **f** 7 14 21 28 35 42 49 56 63   70

2 Each of the following has been made by changing the counting numbers using a **two-step** rule like:

— ⟩ × a number ⟩ —— ⟩ + a number ⟩ —

Find the rule for each.

a 7 12 17 22 27 32 37 42 47 52   **b** 9 19 29 39 49 59 69 79 89 99
c 7 13 19 25 31 37 43 49 55 61   **d** 5   9 13 17 21 25 29 33 37 41
e 7 16 25 34 43 52 61 70 79 88   **f** 10 17 24 31 38 45 52 59 66 73

3 The costs for hiring a car form a pattern.

km	1	2	3	4	5	6	7	8	9	10
Cost (£)	3	5	7	9	11	13	15	17	19	21

Can you find the two-step rule?

Making Formulae

When we can spot a pattern we can make formulae.
Still working with the counting numbers ...

| 1 ostrich | 2 ostriches | 3 ostriches |
| 2 legs | 4 legs | 6 legs |

The number of legs goes up in twos.

> The number of ostriches
> **times 2**
> gives the number of legs.

Check it!

EXERCISE 4

1 Copy and complete the formulae for the following.

a

| 1 stool | 2 stools | 3 stools |
| 3 legs | 6 legs | 9 legs |

> The number of stools
> **times ?**
> gives the number of legs.

b

> The number of spiders
> **times ?**
> gives the number of legs.

| 1 spider | 2 spiders | 3 spiders |
| 8 legs | 16 legs | 24 legs |

c

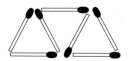

| Picture 1 | Picture 2 | Picture 3 |
| 3 matches | 5 matches | 7 matches |

> The number of the picture
> **times ?**
> **plus ?**
> gives the number
> of matches.

2 Mrs Jones from the furniture shop demonstrates a new design of table.

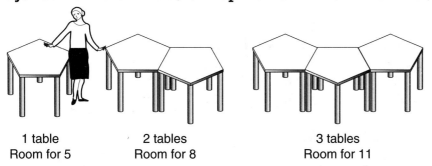

1 table
Room for 5

2 tables
Room for 8

3 tables
Room for 11

a Work out the formula connecting tables to room.

b How many is there room for round 6 tables?

3 Mr Smyth from the same shop prefers the 6-sided tables.

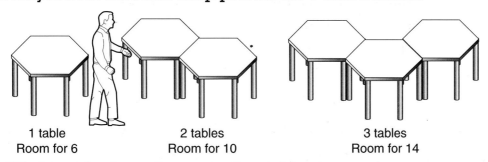

1 table
Room for 6

2 tables
Room for 10

3 tables
Room for 14

a Work out the formula connecting tables to room.

b How many is there room for round 6 tables?

c How many tables do you need if you want to sit 22 people round them?

4

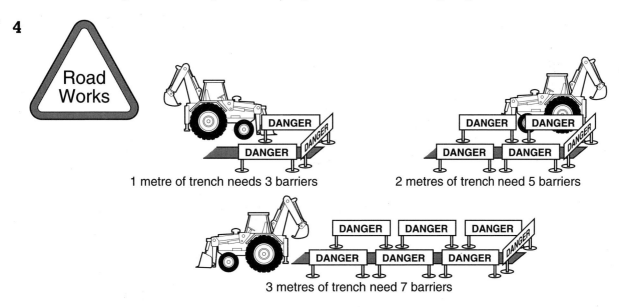

1 metre of trench needs 3 barriers

2 metres of trench need 5 barriers

3 metres of trench need 7 barriers

a Work out a formula to connect the length of trench with the number of barriers.

b How many barriers are needed for 10 metres of trench?

c How many metres of trench can you protect with 51 barriers?

Codes

A code is a way of changing information from one form to another.
The simplest code changes letters for numbers.

A	B	C	D	E	F	G	H	I	J	K	L	M	N	O	P	Q	R	S	T	U	V	W	X	Y	Z
1	2	3	4	5	6	7	8	9	10	11	12	13	14	15	16	17	18	19	20	21	22	23	24	25	26

If we want to write PATTERN, we use the numbers instead: **16 1 20 20 5 18 14**.

Machines can use numbers easier than letters
and this is one reason why we code things.

If we want to keep the message secret, then we can change the
coding numbers by using a secret formula known only to friends.

Example

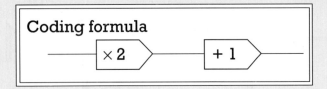

Coding formula

— ×2 > — +1 >

Check that **16 1 20 20 5 18 14** becomes **33 3 41 41 11 37 29**.

Our friend decodes the message by reversing the formula.

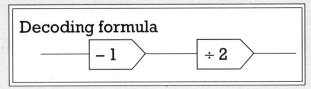

Decoding formula

— −1 > — ÷2 >

reverses order and
reverses the operation.

EXERCISE 5

1 a Put the message 'POST EARLY FOR CHRISTMAS' into the simplest code.
b Now code it further using this formula:

*Post
Early
for
Christmas*

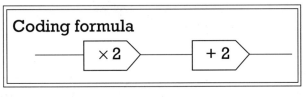

Coding formula

— ×2 > — +2 >

2 Copy this completed crossword grid,
decoding the words as you go.
Use this decoding formula:

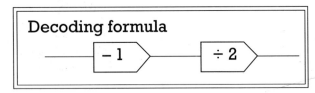

Decoding formula

— −1 > — ÷2 >

37	3	13	41	39
31	■	19	■	17
45	11	29	43	11
11	■	9		9
37	31	39	11	39

3 Here are some coding formulae.
Write the decoding formula for each.

a
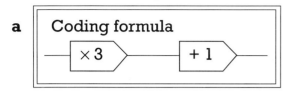
Coding formula
× 3 → + 1

b
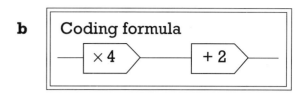
Coding formula
× 4 → + 2

c
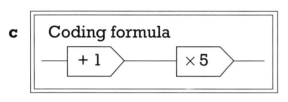
Coding formula
+ 1 → × 5

d
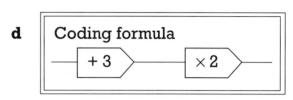
Coding formula
+ 3 → × 2

4 Here is a message and its coding formula.

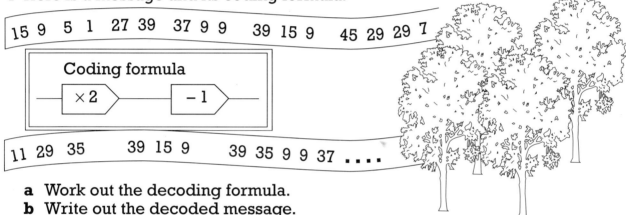

15 9   5 1   27 39   37 9 9   39 15 9   45 29 29 7

Coding formula
× 2 → − 1

11 29 35   39 15 9   39 35 9 9 37 . . . .

a Work out the decoding formula.
b Write out the decoded message.

5 Computers use a very simple coding formula.

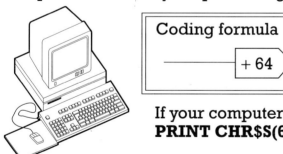

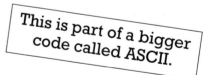
Coding formula
+ 64

This is part of a bigger code called ASCII.

If your computer uses the language BASIC, then
PRINT CHR$S(65) will make the computer print A.

Each of the following commands will make the computer print words.
Decode them to find the words (or type each line into a computer).
a PRINT CHR$(65) + CHR$(68) + CHR$(65) + CHR$(77)
b PRINT CHR$(65) + CHR$(78) + CHR$(68)
c PRINT CHR$(69) + CHR$(86) + CHR$(69)

6 Find out what you can about:

a Braille   **b** Morse   **c** semaphore

and other famous codes.

The Highway
Code

CHECK -UP ON PATTERNS, FORMULAE AND CODES

1 Draw the next picture in this pattern.

 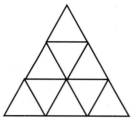

2 Copy and continue these number patterns.

    a 25, 31, 37, 43, 49, ..., ...
    b 209, 207, 205, 203, 201, ..., ...

3 a Make a new pattern with the given rule.

Counting numbers	1	2	3	4	5	6	7	8	9	10
New pattern	7	14								

    b Make a pattern from the first ten counting numbers using this rule:

4 What rule produces these number patterns?

    a 6, 12, 18, 24, 30, 36, ...
    b 3, 5, 7, 9, 11, 13, 15, ... (a two-step rule)

5 Look at these three pictures.

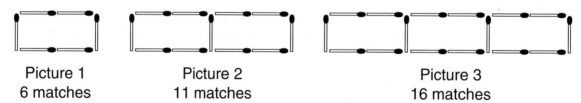

    Picture 1   Picture 2   Picture 3
    6 matches   11 matches   16 matches

    a Draw the next picture.
    b Describe the rule.

> The picture number
> **times ?**
> **add ?**
> gives the number of matches.

6 Here is another design of table from the furniture shop.

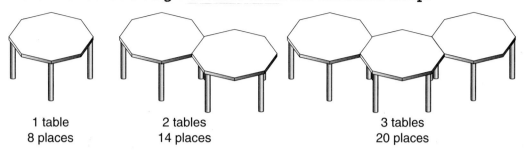

| 1 table | 2 tables | 3 tables |
| 8 places | 14 places | 20 places |

   a Work out the formula connecting the number of tables to the number of places.

   b How many places do you get round 6 tables?

   c How many tables do you need for 32 people?

7 Using the simplest code, what is this word? 3 1 2 9 14

8 This coding formula   ×2   +3

produces this message: | 43 19 21 41 21 41 43 19 13 13 31 11 |

   a What is the decoding formula?

   b What is the message?

7 WAGES

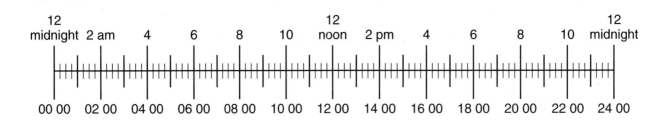

| 12 midnight | 2 am | 4 | 6 | 8 | 10 | 12 noon | 2 pm | 4 | 6 | 8 | 10 | 12 midnight |

00 00   02 00   04 00   06 00   08 00   10 00   12 00   14 00   16 00   18 00   20 00   22 00   24 00

LOOKING BACK

1 a In one year, how many: (i) months   (ii) weeks   (iii) days are there?

  b How many days are in a normal working week?

2 How long is it from:

  a 2 pm to 7 pm

  b 10.30 am to 6.30 pm

  c 09 15 to 14 15

  d 11 20 to 16 50?

Reminders

$$30 \text{ minutes} = \tfrac{1}{2} \text{ hour} = 0.5 \text{ hour}$$

$$15 \text{ minutes} = \tfrac{1}{4} \text{ hour} = 0.25 \text{ hour}$$

$$45 \text{ minutes} = \tfrac{3}{4} \text{ hour} = 0.75 \text{ hour}$$

Example: 7 hours 30 minutes = **7.5 hours**.
(This is useful when using a calculator.)

---

3 Write each of the following in hours:

  a 1 hour 30 minutes   **b** 3 hours 15 minutes   **c** 10 hours 45 minutes

  d 4 hours 30 minutes   **e** six and a half hours   **f** two and a quarter hours

4 Calculate:

  a 5% of £360   **b** 6% of £1240   **c** 12% of £550   **d** 3% of £246

  e 7% of £490   **f** 10% of £25   **g** 9% of £77   **h** 2% of £1483

Fixed Salary

Some people are paid by the year, or by the month or the week.

Their wage does not depend upon how many hours they work.

EXERCISE 1

1 Andrew works as a junior reporter on a local newspaper.
He is paid £450 each month.
How much will he be paid in a year?

2 Sally minds children after school. She earns £15 a day.

  a How much will she earn in a school week?
  b There are 40 weeks in a school year.
     How much will Sally earn in a school year?

3 Zak is a supply teacher. He is paid £84 for
each day he works.

  a In January he worked for 11 days.
     How much did he earn?
  b During the whole year Zak worked 92 days.
     How much did he earn?

4 Leah earns £1420 per month, working in an architect's office
How much will she earn in a year?

5 Tom works in a shop. He earns £140 per week.
He gets paid each week of the year, including holidays.
How much is he paid in a year?

6 Wayne earns £24 000 a year. His wages are paid each month.
How much does he receive each month?

7 Julie earns £300 per week. She works 5 days a week.
How much does she earn each day?

8 Tara is a shop assistant. She earns £3120 per year.
She is paid in 52 equal weekly amounts.
How much is she paid each week?

9 Work out the **annual** salary of each of these people.

a   Olivia
> £185 per week

b   Louis
> £1560 per month

c   Trudy
> £356 per week

10   Mary is paid £165 per week.   Suzie is paid £707 per month.

Who is paid more per year?
(Show **all** your working.)

Hourly Rates

Many people's wages depend upon how many hours they work.
They have a fixed **hourly rate**.

Example

> **Gardener wanted**
>
> 20 hours per week
> Wages: £5.50 per hour
>
> Apply 01756 854234

How much would this gardener
be paid in a week?

In 1 hour he earns £5.50.
So in 20 hours he earns
20 × £5.50 = £110.

Do Worksheet 1

EXERCISE 2

1 Marty is a house painter. He charges £14 an hour for his work.
It takes Marty 8 hours to wallpaper and paint a room.
How much will he earn?

2 Tina is a part-time worker. She works 4 hours on Monday, 3 hours on
Tuesday and 4 hours on Thursday. She is paid £7.50 an hour.
   a Calculate the total number of hours she works in a week.
   b How much is she paid in a week?

3 Bashiri earns £5.62 per hour.
She works from 9 am to 1 pm each day, Monday to Friday.
   a Calculate how many hours she works each day.
   b How many hours does she work in a week?
   c How much does she earn in a week?

4  A carpet-fitter gets paid £9.14 an hour.
He takes five and a half hours to lay new carpets in a house.
How much does he get paid?

Bonus

A bonus is extra money paid to a worker for a job well done,
or as a present at Christmas or holiday time.

5 Terry earns £820 a month working as an assistant in a chemist's.
His employer is pleased with his work.
She gives Terry a £50 bonus at Christmas.
What is Terry's total pay for December?

6  Janna is paid £112 a week.

   a How much is this a year?

Her boss gave her a £35 holiday bonus.
He also gave her a £40 bonus at Christmas.

   b How much money did Janna get altogether in the year?

7 Simon works in a factory making lamp-shades.
He is paid £4.35 an hour. He works 35 hours a week.

   a Calculate Simon's basic weekly wage.
   b Simon is paid a £10 bonus each week if he makes more
than 200 lamp-shades.
How much would Simon earn in a week when he made
210 lamp-shades?

Time-sheets

People often have to 'clock in' and 'clock out' of work.
This allows you to work out the hours a person has worked.
Here is part of a time-sheet.

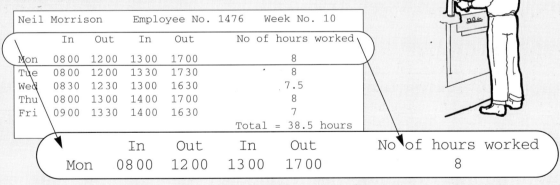

Neil Morrison   Employee No. 1476   Week No. 10

	In	Out	In	Out	No of hours worked
Mon	0800	1200	1300	1700	8
Tue	0800	1200	1330	1730	8
Wed	0830	1230	1300	1630	7.5
Thu	0800	1300	1400	1700	8
Fri	0900	1330	1400	1630	7
				Total =	38.5 hours

	In	Out	In	Out	No of hours worked
Mon	0800	1200	1300	1700	8

Look at Monday.
Neil arrived at 8 am and left for lunch at 12 noon.   **4 hours**
He then came back at 1 pm and worked until 5 pm.   **4 hours**
Neil worked **8 hours** on Monday.

EXERCISE 3

1 On Tuesday, Sue arrived at work at 9 am and left for lunch at 1 pm.

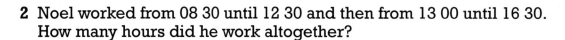

   a How many hours did she work?

She came back at 2 pm and worked until 5 pm.

   b How many hours did she work after lunch?
   c How many hours did she work altogether that day?

2 Noel worked from 08 30 until 12 30 and then from 13 00 until 16 30.
How many hours did he work altogether?

3  Catriona has a half day on a Wednesday.
She comes in to work at 7.45 am and works until 12.15 pm.

How many hours does she work on a Wednesday?

4 Zahir works for 4 hours on Thursday.
He came in to work at 10 am.

When did he finish work?

5 Andrea works for four and a half hours each day.
She comes in to work at 8.15 am.

When does she finish work for the day?

6 This is part of Sallyanne's time-sheet.

When did she finish work that Friday?

	In	Out	In	Out	No of hours worked
Fri	07 00	12 00	13 00		8

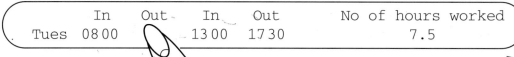

7 This is Heather's time-sheet.

	In	Out	In	Out	No of hours worked
Tues	08 00		13 00	17 30	7.5

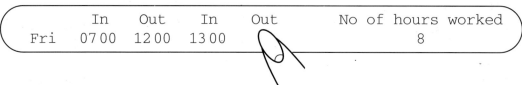

When did she leave for lunch?

Do Worksheet 2

Overtime

Any extra hours a person works are called **overtime**.
Normally, you are paid more per hour for overtime.

Double time

If overtime is paid at 'double time', you get paid double the hourly rate.

Example

Normal rate of pay = £4.20 per hour.
Overtime at double time = £4.20 × 2 = £8.40 per hour.

Do
Worksheet
3

EXERCISE 4

1  Shamindar works as a joiner. His basic wage in £8 per hour.
He is paid double time for any overtime he does.

   a Calculate his overtime rate.
   b One week he works 5 hours of overtime.
      How much will he be paid for his overtime?

2 Tracey has a basic hourly wage of £6.20.
She is paid double time for any overtime she does.

   a What is her overtime rate?
   b She works 7 hours of overtime.
      How much will she be paid for doing it?

3 Harry's boss asks him to work 6 hours of overtime.
He says he will pay Harry double time.
Harry's usual hourly rate is £5.40.

How much will Harry get for doing the overtime?

4 Andy does some overtime one Monday evening.
Here is part of his time-sheet.

   a How many hours of overtime does he work?
   b Overtime is paid at double the usual £7.20 rate.
      How much will Andy be paid for working overtime on Monday?

	In	Out
Mon	1830	2130

5 Helena does overtime from 6 pm until 9 pm on Monday,
Tuesday and Thursday.

   a How many hours of overtime does she do in a week?
   b Overtime is paid at double time.
      Her normal hourly rate is £4.80.
      What is her overtime pay each week?

Do
Worksheet
4

Piece Work

Some people are paid a set amount each
time they make or do something.
This is called **piece work**.

Example

Tess hand-paints models.
She is paid £1.20 for each model she paints.
She paints 50 models in a week.

How much will she be paid?

Tess's wage = 50 × £1.20 = £60

EXERCISE 5

1 Nazir makes bird-tables. He is paid £4 for each bird-table he makes.

  a One week he makes 12 bird-tables.
     How much will he earn?

  b The next week he makes 9 bird-tables.
     How much will he earn that week?

2 Margaret works from home. She is paid
50 pence for every soft toy she sews together.
In one week she sews 42 teddies. How much will she earn?

3 Ellie makes hand-made pottery vases for
a local company. She is paid £3.50 for each
vase she makes. On Monday she makes 5 vases,
on Tuesday 2, on Wednesday 4, on Thursday 5
and on Friday 6.

  a How many vases did she make in the week?
  b How much will she be paid?

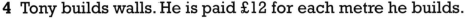

4 Tony builds walls. He is paid £12 for each metre he builds.

  a Tony builds 5 metres of wall one day.
     How much will he be paid?
  b Tony builds 28 metres of wall in the whole week.
     What would Tony's wage be for that week?
  c One day Tony earned £36 for building walls.
     How many metres of wall did he build?

5 A company pays its employees to sell insurance over the phone.
An employee is paid 15 pence for each phone call she makes.
One evening Tracey phoned 58 people. How much did she earn?

6 Pankja, Rowan and Emily work in a factory that makes jeans.
They all do different jobs.
Pankja cuts out the material for the jeans.
Rowan sews the jeans together.
Emily puts the zips into the jeans.
The table shows how many pairs of jeans each does in one week.

	Mon	Tues	Wed	Thurs	Fri	Rate per pair
Pankja	45	49	42	51	47	60p
Rowan	27	28	25	28	30	75p
Emily	54	47	48	47	42	62p

a Work out how many pairs of jeans each person did in the week.
b How much did each person earn in the week?
c Who earned the most?

7  Liam folds jumpers and puts them into bags.
He is paid £8.40 for every bundle of 20 jumpers he does.
In one day he folds and packs 140 jumpers.

a How many bundles of 20 jumpers did he do?
b How much will he be paid?

✩ Commission

> The more you sell, the more you are paid!

This is called being paid **commission**.

Example Tom sells cars. He is paid £20 for every £1000 worth he sells.
Tom sells a car for £6000.
How much will he be paid?

> Tom's pay
> He sells 6000 ÷ 1000 = 6 lots of £1000
> His pay is 6 × £20 = £120.

EXERCISE 6

1 Bonita sells cosmetics. She is paid £8 for every £100 of cosmetics she sells.
One week Bonita sold £900 of cosmetics.
a How many lots of £100 are her sales worth?
b How much commission is she paid?

2 Charlotte sells books. She is paid £9 for every £200 worth
of books she sells. Charlotte works hard one week.
She sells £1400 worth of books. How much will she earn?

⭐ Commission is Usually a Percentage of Sales

Example

Better Books
Commission:
2% of all sales

Michael sells £850
worth of books.

Michael's wage
Commission = 2% of £850
= 0.02 × £850
= £17

EXERCISE 6B

1 Patrick sells £280 worth of clothes.
His boss pays him 5% commission on his sales.
How much does Patrick earn?

2 In one week Corey sold £750 worth of windows.
His commission is 4% of his sales.
How much will Corey earn that week?

WEATHERWISE
WINDOWS

3 Work out the commission due to each of these employees.

	Employee	Commission	Value of sales
a	A. Baker	3% of sales	£1200
b	B. Kahn	5% of sales	£330
c	J. Green	7% of sales	£586
d	K. Reeves	1% of sales	£14 240

4 Leon works in a shop selling electrical goods.
In one day he sells
a TV worth   £480,
a fridge worth   £275,
washing machines worth   £540 and £660,
and a tumble dryer worth £245.

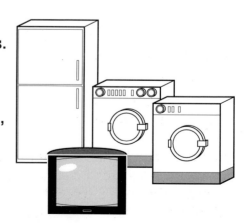

a What is the total value of his sales?

Leon is paid 3% commission on his sales.
b How much is Leon paid?

Deductions

Some money is removed from your wages before you get them.

National Insurance: this is around 6% of your wage
(a safeguard against illness or job loss).

Income Tax: this is more complicated, but you can estimate
about 19% of your wage (money needed for running the country).

Pension Fund: this is not compulsory and is usually
around 6% of your wage (for your old age).

Other deductions can include union dues, council tax, BUPA payments, rent,
and many other things which can be paid direct before you get your wage.

Example   Jean earns £2000 before deductions.
How much does she take home if she has deductions
for national insurance, income tax and her pension?

National insurance   6% of £2000 = £120
Income tax   19% of £2000 = £380
Pension   6% of £2000 = £120
Total deductions   = £620
Net pay   £2000 – £620 = **£1380**

Jean takes home £1380.

EXERCISE 7

1 Calculate the national insurance deductions on a wage of:
   a £900   **b** £580   **c** £2500   **d** £1750   **e** £1390

2 Estimate the amount of income tax due on a wage of:
   a £800   **b** £640   **c** £3000   **d** £1560   **e** £12 000

3 Work out the pension contributions on a wage of:
   a £600   **b** £720   **c** £560   **d** £1300   **e** £1800

4 Peter earns £1800 a month but has to pay
   for a pension, national insurance and tax.

   Calculate:
   a the total deductions
   b his take-home pay.

5 Angela earns £2500 a month. As well as paying national insurance, tax and
   a pension, she has a council tax payment of £50, a car payment of £10 and
   £3 union dues deducted from her wage.
   Calculate her take-home pay.

CHECK-UP ON WAGES

1 Richard works 35 hours a week as a joiner.
He is paid £7.50 per hour.

How much is he paid in a week?

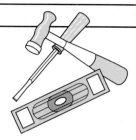

2 This is part of Chloe's time-sheet. She earns £5.20 per hour.

	In	Out	In	Out
Tuesday 14th	8.30 am	12.30 pm	1.30 pm	5 pm

Calculate:
a how many hours Chloe works on Tuesday
b how much she is paid.

3  Kevin Gibson is a digger operator.
His basic rate of pay is £4.80.
He is paid double time for any overtime he does.
Kevin works 5 hours of overtime.
How much will he be paid for the overtime?

4 Amber McGee is an artist.
She sells pictures to a local shop.
She is paid £3.50 for each picture.
Amber sells 24 pictures in one month.
How much is she paid?

5  Joanna Swanson designs and makes
ear-rings to sell to a craft shop. She is paid
£15 for every 6 pairs of ear-rings. Joanna
made 48 pairs of ear-rings one week.

How much money did she receive?

 6 Cameron Bennett is a salesman. He has a basic wage of £160 per week.
He is also paid 4% commission on his sales.
His sales one week were worth £4500.
a Work out how much commission Cameron gets.
b How much would he be paid altogether?

7  Anuradi earns £1200 a month.
a Calculate: (i) her pension payment (at 6%)
(ii) her national insurance payment (at 6%).
b Estimate the income tax due (at 19%).
c Calculate her take-home pay.

8 BEARINGS AND SCALE DRAWINGS

LOOKING BACK

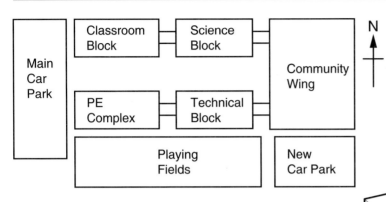

1 This is a plan of Mains Academy.
What lies:

a north of the technical block?
b north-east of the PE complex?
c south-west of the community wing?

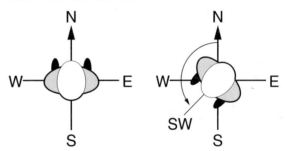

2 Angie is facing north.
She turns clockwise to face east.

3 Ryan is facing north.
He turns anticlockwise to
face south-west.

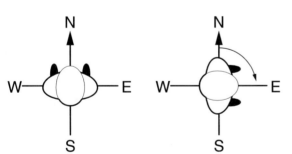

Find the angle turned by Angie.

Find the angle turned by Ryan.

4 What turn is needed?

a I'm facing **north.**
I want to face
east.

b I'm facing **west.**
I want to face
south-west.

5 **a** Make an accurate copy of this triangle.
b What is the size of the side BC?
c Use a protractor to measure ∠BCA and ∠ABC.

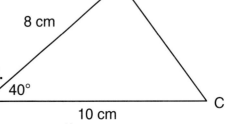

Halving and Doubling

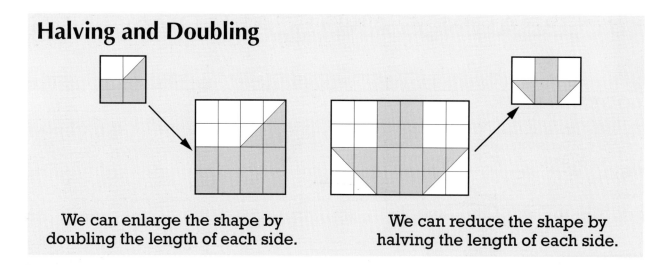

We can enlarge the shape by doubling the length of each side.

We can reduce the shape by halving the length of each side.

EXERCISE 1

1 Enlarge these shapes by doubling the length of each side.
(Use 1 cm squared paper.)

Artists often use this trick to enlarge pictures.

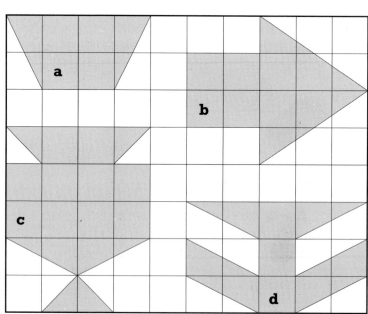

2 Enlarge these shapes by doubling the length of each side.

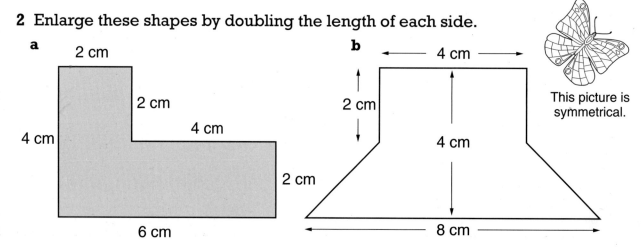

This picture is symmetrical.

3 Reduce these shapes by halving the length of each side.

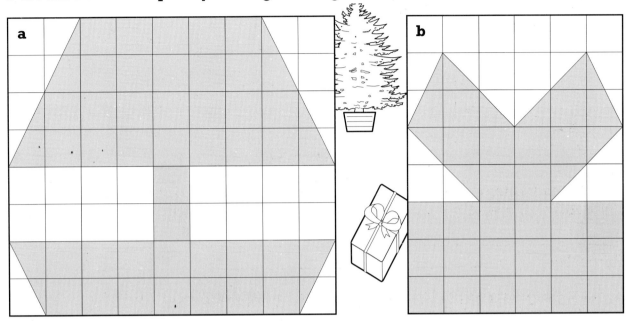

4 Reduce these shapes by halving the length of each side.

a

8 cm

4 cm   4 cm

8 cm

b

6 cm

4 cm

2 cm

 5 These shapes have been drawn on a 1 cm grid.
  a Find the area of each shape.
  b Enlarge the shapes by doubling their sides.
  c Find the area of each of the shapes you have drawn.
  d What do you notice about the areas?

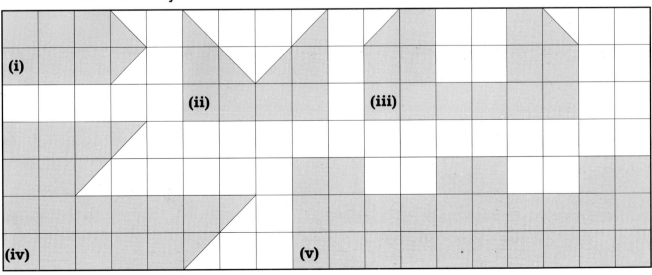

(i)

(ii)

(iii)

(iv)

(v)

Similar Rectangles

Original length ———[× 1.5]——— New length

Original breadth ———[× 1.5]——— New breadth

| The sizes have been changed by the same factor. The rectangles are similar. |

'The Balloonist' in a 4 × 6 frame.

'The Balloonist' in a 6 × 9 frame.

Original length ———[× 0.67]——— New length

Original breadth ———[× 1]——— New breadth

'The Balloonist' in a 4 × 4 frame.

| The sizes have been changed by different factors. This rectangle is not similar to the others. |

EXERCISE 2

1 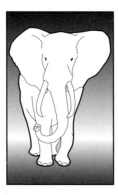 This photograph is a 7 cm × 11 cm rectangle.

a A similar rectangle is made using this machine:

———[× 3]———

What is the length and breadth of this new rectangle?

b A poster-sized print is made using this machine:

———[× 12]———

Work out its dimensions.

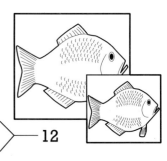

2 A rectangular tile has a length of 4.5 cm. Its breadth is 4 cm.

a Draw the enlargement machine if the breadth is enlarged to 12 cm.

b What is the length of the new tile?

4 ———[× ?]——— 12

3

An art gallery sells large and small posters of some famous works of art.

Actual size —| × 0.8 |⟩— Large poster size

Actual size —| × 0.2 |⟩— Small poster size

Work out the sizes of the following as:

(i) large posters   (ii) small posters.

a a painting 2 metres by 3 metres

b an etching 60 cm by 80 cm

c a portrait 150 cm by 100 cm

4 A photograph which is 15 cm wide by 20 cm long is used for a stamp.
The stamp is only 3 cm wide.

a Draw the machine used to shrink the photo.

15 —| ÷ ? |⟩— 3

b Work out the length of the stamp.
c The diagonal of the photo measures 25 cm. How long is the diagonal of the stamp?

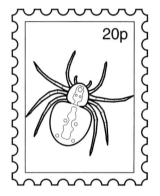

5

A famous painting was stolen.
The newspapers wanted its photo on the front page.
The original was 50 cm wide × 90 cm long.
The width of the photo was 10 cm.

a Draw the machine needed to shrink the painting.

b Work out the length of the photo on the front page.

6 Find two different sizes of a picture and check by measurement that the same enlargement machine has been used.

Using a Plan

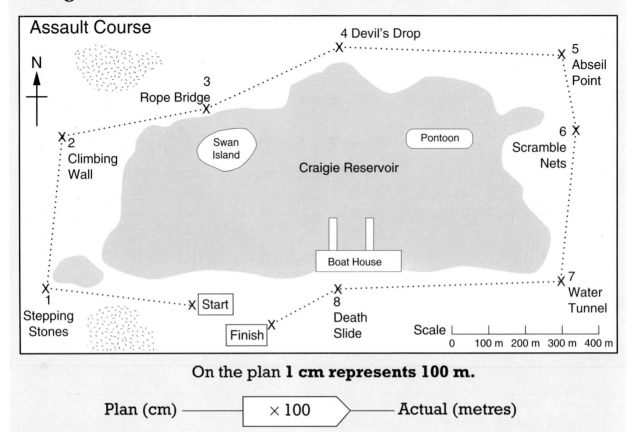

Assault Course

4 Devil's Drop

5 Abseil Point

3 Rope Bridge

2 Climbing Wall

Swan Island

Pontoon

Craigie Reservoir

6 Scramble Nets

Boat House

1 Stepping Stones

Start

Finish

8 Death Slide

7 Water Tunnel

Scale
0   100 m   200 m   300 m   400 m

On the plan 1 cm represents 100 m.

Plan (cm) ——————[× 100 >—————— Actual (metres)

EXERCISE 3

1 a What is the actual distance between the rope bridge and Devil's Drop?
 b What is the actual shortest distance between the death slide and the stepping stones?
 c Which obstacle lies directly north of the death slide?
 d Which obstacle lies north-east of the stepping stones?
 e What is the actual distance between the water tunnel and the death slide?

2 Sushila and her classmates are trying out the assault course.
 How far will they run to complete the whole course?

3 A model railway club provided this plan of The Puffin' Bobby.

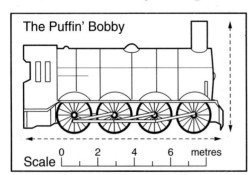

The Puffin' Bobby

Scale
0   2   4   6   metres

On the plan **1 cm represents 2 m.**

plan (cm) ——————[× 2 >—————— actual (metres)

 a What is the actual:
  (i) length (ii) height of the locomotive?
 b What is the diameter of the wheels on the actual engine?
 c The boiler is actually 3 metres long.
  How long will it be on the plan?

4 This plan shows an orienteering course.
1 cm represents 1 km. Leg 1 measures 8 cm. It points west.
So leg 1 is a run of **8 km west**. Describe the rest of the course in this way.

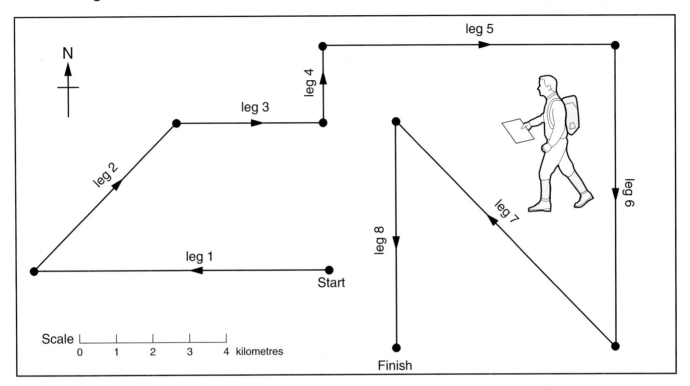

5 Make a plan like the one in question **4** to show this orienteering course.
Use a scale of **1 cm to 1 km**.

Journey	Direction	Distance
1st leg	West	4 km
2nd leg	North	8 km
3rd leg	East	3 km
4th leg	South-east	5 km
5th leg	East	2 km
6th leg	South	3.5 km
7th leg	West	4.5 km

6 A rectangular piece of land measures
1 km by 1.5 km.
It has been made available for use as a
9-hole golf course.

a Use a suitable scale to draw up your
own plans for this course.
b Write out the nine legs of the course
like the above routes.

Three-figure Bearings

Remember

We can describe direction using angle only.

We measure the angle from **north.**

We **always** measure **clockwise**.

The three-figure bearing for **north is 000°**.

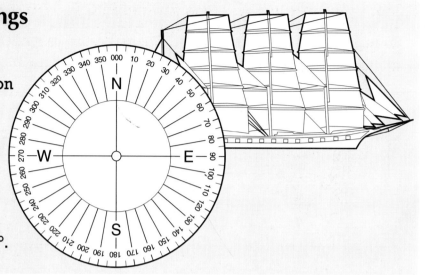

EXERCISE 4

Use the diagram above to help you answer these questions.

1 What is the three-figure bearing for:

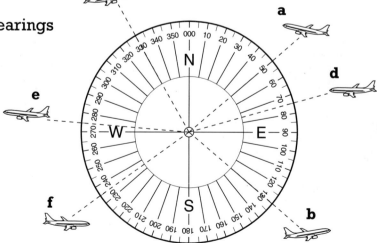

   a south?   **b** north-east?   **c** west?

   d north-west?   **e** east?   **f** south-east?

2 What **compass direction** do these bearings represent?

   a 135°   **b** 000°   **c** 270°   **d** 045°   **e** 315°   **f** 090°

3 A plane is flying **north.**
What will be its new **compass direction** after a turn of:

   a 90° clockwise   **b** 45° anticlockwise

   c 135° clockwise   **d** 90° anticlockwise?

4 Record the three-figure bearings of these aircraft.

5 John measures the bearings of different things in the park.
Write down the three-figure bearing of:

a the café   **b** the boating pond   **c** the football pitch
d the putting green   **e** the picnic area   **f** the tennis courts

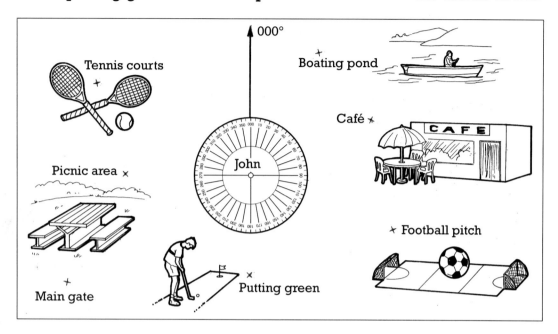

6 A course has been designed for the Mid-summer Rally.
Copy and complete the table to describe the course.

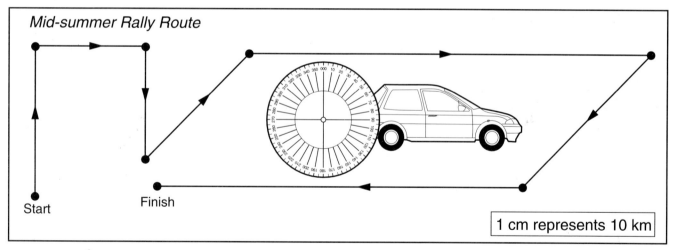

1 cm represents 10 km

Journey	Direction	Bearing	Distance
1st leg	North	000°	40 km
2nd leg			
3rd leg			
4th leg			
5th leg			
6th leg			
7th leg			

EXERCISE 5

1 The harbour master keeps track of ships' movements by radar.
Copy and complete the table to give the bearing and distance of all the ships from the harbour.

Ship	Bearing	Distance
Gwent	020°	25 km
Dart		
Arthur		
Rocket		
Merlin		
Shark		
Stingray		

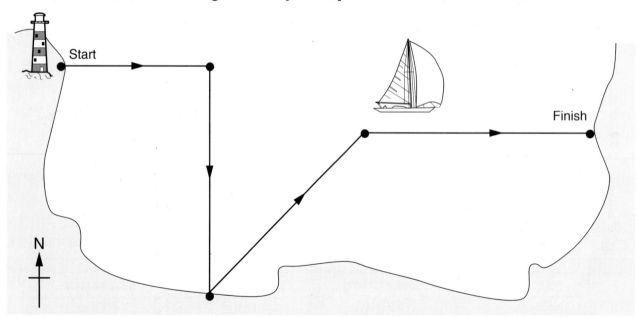

2 A yacht worked its way across the bay as shown.
  a Describe this journey using bearings and distances.
    1 cm represents 1 km.
  b What was the total length of the journey?

3 A boat's skipper records his journey like this:
  6 km on a bearing of 090°,
  then 4 km on a bearing of 000°,
  then 5 km on a bearing of 200°.

  Make a plan of this journey.
  Use a scale of 1 cm to 1 km.

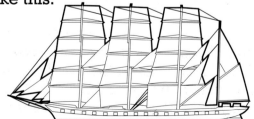

CHECK-UP ON BEARINGS AND SCALE DRAWINGS

1 This shape is drawn on a 1 cm grid.

Enlarge the shape by doubling
the length of the sides.

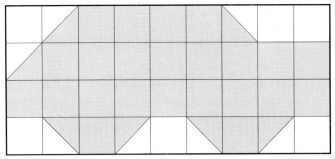

2 The latch forms a rectangle which is 25 cm × 10 cm.

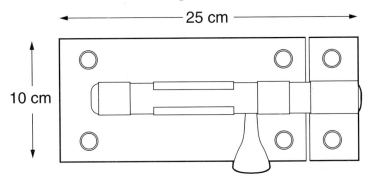

25 cm

10 cm

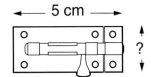

5 cm

?

A similar rectangular latch is used by model makers. The length of it is 5 cm.

a Copy and complete the machine used to shrink the latch.

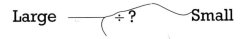

Large ──── ÷ ? ──── Small

b How wide is the model latch?

3 Here is a map of the top end of Scott Street.

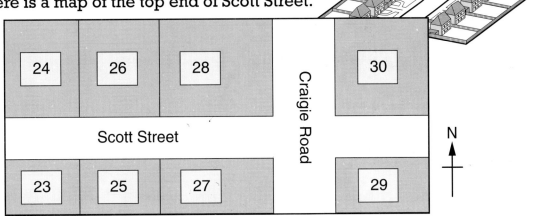

| 24 | 26 | 28 | | 30 |

Craigie Road

Scott Street

| 23 | 25 | 27 | | 29 |

N

a Which house lies to the north of number 29?
b Which house lies to the north-east of number 27?
c Which house lies to the south-west of number 28?
d Amy lives at number 24.
In what direction does she travel to visit her friend at number 25?

4 This is a plan of an orienteering course.
1 cm represents 100 m on the plan.

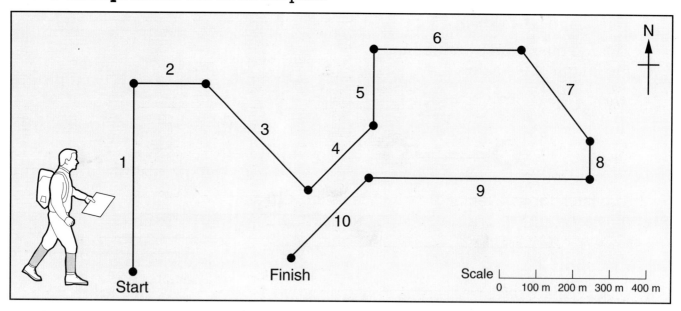

Copy and complete the table to describe the course.

Stage	Distance	Direction	Bearing
1	500 m	N	000°
2			
3			

5 The radar at a harbour shows six ships.

a Which ship is on a bearing of 270°?

b What is the bearing and distance of the *Yamaha*?

c Which ship is furthest away?

d What is the bearing and distance of the *Bemar*?

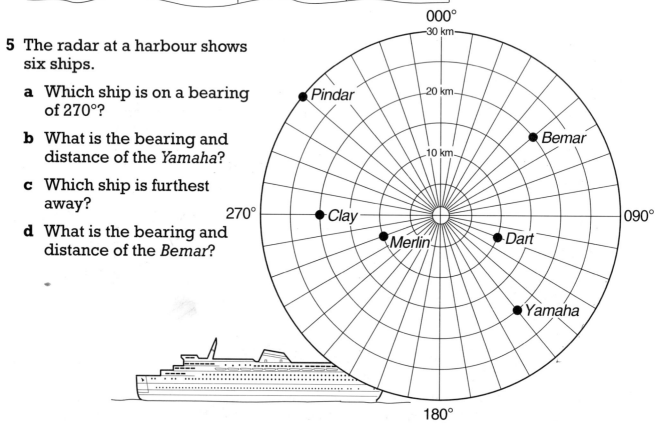

9 BANKING MONEY

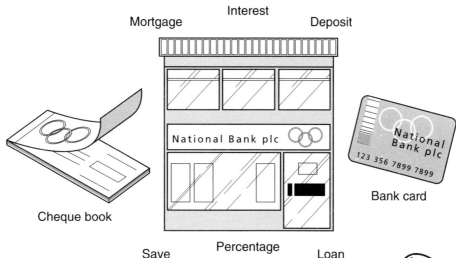

Mortgage · Interest · Deposit

National Bank plc

Bank card

Cheque book

Save · Percentage · Loan

LOOKING BACK

1 Neil is counting his money.
He has £53 in the bank and £20 in cash at home.

How much money does he have altogether?

2
Jan's mother is buying a car from a garage.
It costs her £3672.
She borrows £3500 and pays the rest in cash.

How much does she pay in cash?

3 Written as a vulgar fraction, $6\% = \frac{6}{100}$.
Write each of these percentages in a similar way.
a 9% **b** 14% **c** 97% **d** 3% **e** 1% **f** 10%

4 Written as a decimal fraction, $6\% = 0.06$.
Write the following percentages as decimal fractions.
a 24% **b** 46% **c** 35% **d** 12% **e** 7% **f** 1% **g** 10%

5 A department store has a sale after Christmas.

Calculate 75% of £16.

CDs now only
75%
of marked price

£16

6 A shop has to increase its prices.

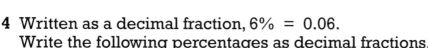

Increase 5%

Camera £95

Video recorder £220

Increase 2%

a Work out the increase on: (i) the camera (ii) the video machine.
b Work out the new price for: (i) the camera (ii) the video machine.

Bank Accounts

At some time in your life you will use a bank. Most employers pay your wages directly into your bank account.

There are two main kinds of bank accounts:

Current account
- This is for day-to-day use.
- You get a cheque book and a bank card.
- You can pay bills, buy shopping, etc., without carrying large sums of money about.
- Every month you get a **statement**.
  It says how much money you have left.
- You can use the 'hole in the wall' machine outside the bank.
- You may overdraw (take out more than you have), but the bank will charge you interest.

Deposit account
- This is a good way to save money.
- You get a bank book.
- The book is updated whenever you put money in or take money out.
- Every year you receive **interest**.
- Interest can vary from bank to bank.
  It is a good idea to shop around.
- You can get a card to let you use the 'hole in the wall'.

'In the red' means being overdrawn.
'In the black' means you have money in your account.

The Cheque Book

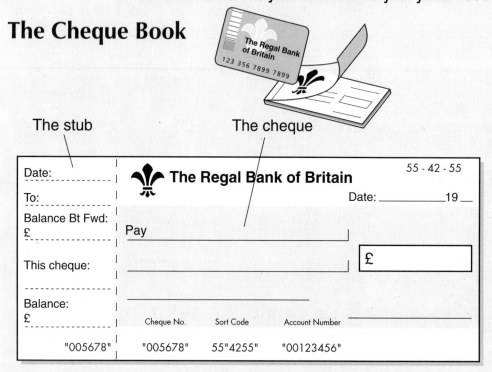

The stub

The cheque

Date:				
To:				
Balance Bt Fwd: £				
This cheque:				
Balance: £				

The Regal Bank of Britain

55 - 42 - 55

Date: _____ 19 __

Pay _____

£ _____

| | Cheque No. | Sort Code | Account Number | |
| "005678" | "005678" | 55"4255" | "00123456" | |

Writing Cheques

Andrew Hanna has a balance of £284.26 in his current account.
He wrote a cheque to Scot Fuel for £48.90. His new balance is £235.36.

Date: _17/5/96_		**The Regal Bank of Britain**	55 - 42 - 55
To: _Scot Fuel_			Date: _17/5_ 19_96_
Balance Bt Fwd: £ _284.26_		Pay _Scot Fuel Company_	
This cheque: _£48.90_		_Forty-eight Pounds and ninety pence_	£ _48.90—_
Balance: £ _235.36_			_Andrew Hanna_
		Cheque No. Sort Code Account Number	
"005678"	"005678"	55"4255" "00123456"	

He fills in the stub to keep a record. (Make sure it is correct.)
He writes the amount in words and figures.
He tears off the cheque and gives it to Scot Fuel.
The stub remains in his cheque book.

Get Worksheet **1**

EXERCISE 1

Write cheques for the following bills and purchases.
Complete the stub on each cheque.
Make sure you work out the new balance
on each stub.
Start with a balance of **£235.**
Sign your cheques with your own name if you wish.

	Date	To	Amount
1	19th May	Marts and Sparts	£25.00
2	21st May	Safeworld	£17.38
3	23rd May	Young's Garage	£15.00
4	26th May	Brown's Newsagent	£5.76
5	29th May	Eastern Electric	£49.74
6	30th May	Border Insurance	£12.38

Keeping the Balance

What's in your bank account is called the **balance**.
Dave has a balance of £90.
He signs a cheque for £100.
We say his account is overdrawn by £10.

In the olden days, this £10 would be recorded in red ink,
which is why we talk about being 'in the red'.
Normal entries were made in black ink, so 'in the black'
means there is money in the account.

Solvent is another word for having money in your account.

EXERCISE 2

1  Bethia has £95 in her current account.
She writes three cheques: £15 for petrol, £29 for groceries
and £26 for clothes.

How much money has she left in her account?

2 Joe has £62 in his account.
He has five bills to pay: £13, £8, £15, £4 and £8.

  a Does he have enough money to pay for these bills?
  b How much is left over, if any?

3  To start with, Phil had £180 in the bank.
He wrote a cheque for a garage bill of £129.
He later took £50 out of his account with his bank card.

How much has he left?

4 Nadine had £105 in her bank.
She wrote a £55 cheque for her rent.
She then wrote cheques for £10 at the Record Shop
and £25 in the Clothes Rack.

How much has she left?

5 Fadi has £78 in his current account.
He writes cheques for £63 and £24.

By how much is he overdrawn?

6

Jon has £75 in his current account.
He has four bills to pay:

> £22 for insurance,
> £38 for electricity,
> £17 for his car,
> £3 for newspapers.

a If he pays all his bills, is he still solvent or is he in the red?
b If so, by how much?

7 Ruth has a bank balance of £605.
She writes a cheque for £310 to pay
for her holiday flight and £286 for her
holiday accommodation.
How much more can she spend before
going into the red?

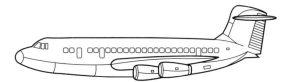

8

Rachel wants to buy a ghettoblaster.
It costs £80.
She has a bank balance of £57.

How much should she pay into her
account to stay solvent?

9 Jim gets a ministatement using his bank card.
By how much is he overdrawn?

The Regal Bank of Britain

	Withdrawal	Balance
		£216.73
Cheque	£ 75.89	
Cheque	£158.31	

Thank you for using The Regal Bank of Britain

10 Complete the statements on Worksheet 2 by filling in the
blank boxes.

Get
Worksheet
2

Rates of Interest

Money kept in a deposit account for a year will gain interest.

| 5% **p.a.** or 5% **per annum** both mean 5% **a year**. |

Example   Gemma leaves £30 in her bank for a year.
The bank pays interest at 5% p.a.

How much interest does Gemma get?

Calculate 5% of £30.
On the calculator   5 ÷ 100 × 30 = ┌──────┐ **1.5**

So Gemma receives £1.50 interest.
The balance in her account is £30 + £1.50 = £31.50.

EXERCISE 3

1 Calculate:
  a 6% of £40   **b** 9% of £25   **c** 4% of £16   **d** 8% of £120
  e 16% of £1000 **f** 1% of £3   **g** 78% of £30 000 **h** 53% of £100 000

2 Pat is given £150 for her birthday.
She decides to put it into a deposit
account in the National Bank.

  a How much interest will she get
    at the end of the year?
  b How much will be in the bank then?

┌─────────────────────────────┐
│ NATIONAL BANK   │
│ Deposit Account Interest Rate │
│   **8% p.a.**   │
└─────────────────────────────┘

3    Frank leaves £200 in the National Bank for a year.

  a How much interest will he get?
  b What will his balance be then?

4 Mary gets 8% p.a. on savings of £600.

  a How much interest will she get after a year?
  b Calculate her balance after the interest is added.

5 Work out a year's interest for each of the following:
  a £600 at 8% p.a   **b** £500 at 4% p.a.   **c** £3500 at 7% p.a.
  d £550 at 6% p.a.   **e** £400 at 10% p.a.   **f** £2400 at 9% p.a.

6 Work out the amount that is in the bank once interest has been added.
  a £500 at 7% p.a.   **b** £850 at 6% p.a.   **c** £3000 at 8% p.a.
  d £650 at 5% p.a.   **e** £600 at 4% p.a.   **f** £5000 at 3% p.a.

The Bank Book

A deposit account bank book keeps a record of:
- all the money put into the account (deposits)
- all the money removed from the account (debits)
- all the interest.

Example

Date	Code	Deposit	Debit	Balance
12/7/95	Cash	£500		£500
12/7/96	Interest at 6%	£30		£530
18/8/96	Cheque		£100	£430

EXERCISE 3B

REGAL BANK
Deposit Account Interest Rate
6% p.a.

1 Elaine got £50 for her birthday.
  She decided to put it into a deposit account in the Regal Bank.
  Here is Elaine's bank book:

Date	Code	Deposit	Debit	Balance
17/5/95	Cash	£50		£50
17/5/96	Interest	£3		£53

  a Check that the interest is correct.
  b Check that the balance is correct.

2 Her friend Marie got £100 for her birthday.
  She decided to put her money in a deposit account with the Regal Bank.
  Copy and complete this bit of Marie's bank book.

Date	Code	Deposit	Debit	Balance
28/6/95	Cash	£100		£100
28/6/96	Interest	?		?

3 Clive's bank book is shown here. Calculate the value of: **a** A **b** B **c** C

Date	Code	Deposit	Debit	Balance
12/7/95	Cash	£800		£800
12/7/96	Interest at 6%	A		B
18/8/96	Cheque		£250	C

Do Worksheet **3**

Decimal Interest Rates

Barry receives 8.5% p.a. interest.
He has £74 in his savings account.
The bank teller shows Barry how the computer uses
a number machine to work out the interest.

$$8.5 \div 100 = 0.085$$

Amount £74 ⟶ Rate ×0.085 ⟶ Interest £6.29

$$0.085 + 1$$

Another machine works out the balance after a year.

Amount £74 ⟶ ×1.085 ⟶ Balance £80.29

EXERCISE 3C

1 Phil puts £60 in the bank.
He gets 6.4% interest at the end of the year.

   a Use this machine to work out the interest.

   Amount £60 ⟶ Rate ×0.064 ⟶ Interest [ ]

   b Use this machine to work out the balance.

   Amount £60 ⟶ ×1.064 ⟶ Balance [ ]

2 Aisling puts £94 birthday money in a savings account.
At the end of the year she gets 7.5% interest.
   a Draw a number machine to calculate her interest. (Hint: 7.5 ÷ 100.)
   b Draw a number machine to calculate the balance. (Hint: add 1.)

3  Joanna puts £200 in a deposit account.
The rate of interest is 8.2% p.a.
Use a number machine to find how much money
Joanna will have in the bank at the end of a year.

4 Moira and Matt are twins.
They decide to open a joint bank account.
They each put in £100. The rate of interest is 9.4%.
   a Draw a machine to calculate how much interest
      they will get at the end of the year.
   b They decide to lift the interest and share it.
      How much will each one get?

Do Worksheet 4   Do Worksheet 5

Borrowing Money

You can borrow money from a bank to buy certain items.
The bank will charge you interest.
The rates of interest you will be charged vary from bank to bank.
You should shop around.

This ready reckoner shows the **monthly repayments** on a loan of £1000
for different rates of interest and for different lengths of time.

Period of loan	Interest rates		
	8%	9%	10%
Months	£	£	£
12	87	87.50	88
24	45	45.70	46
36	31	31.80	32
42	27.30	27.80	28
48	24.40	24.90	25.40

To borrow £1000

Example 1 To borrow £1000 at 9% for 24 months costs you £45.70 per month.

Example 2 To borrow £5000 at 9% for 24 months costs you
$5 \times £45.70 = £228.50$ per month.

EXERCISE 4

1 Use the above table to find the monthly repayments on:
- **a** £1000 at 9% for 48 months
- **b** £1000 at 10% for 42 months
- **c** £5000 at 8% for 24 months
- **d** £10 000 at 10% for 36 months
- **e** £7000 at 8% for 12 months
- **f** £2000 at 8% for 12 months

> **Example: finding the total cost of a loan**
> £1000 at 9% for 24 months costs you £45.70 **per month**.
> So the total cost of the loan = $£45.70 \times 24 = £1096.80$.

2 Calculate the total cost of each loan in question **1**.

3 Calculate the cost of the loans for these items.

£3000 at 8% for 24 months

£5000 at 10% for 42 months

£4000 at 9% for 12 months

Getting a Mortgage

A **mortgage** is a large loan taken over a long time.
Many people need one to help them buy their house.

Example

Mark and Sally see a house which costs £40 000.

The bank says it will lend them 95% of the money.
The rest they will have to provide as a **deposit**.
This means they will need to find 5% of £40 000.

$$5 \div 100 \times £40\ 000 = £2000$$

Mark and Sally will need to pay £2000 as a deposit.

EXERCISE 5

1 Calculate the deposit for these amounts if
you get a 95% loan:

  a £36 000   **b** £54 000   **c** £22 000

  d £48 000   **e** £100 000   **f** £8500

2 Another bank offers clients a 90% loan for buying houses.
  a What percentage is needed as a deposit?
  b Calculate the deposits for these amounts if you get a 90% loan:
    (i) £43 000   (ii) £76 000   (iii) £61 000
    (iv) £58 000   (v) £39 000

3 Sally asks 'What will be the monthly payments?'
The bank manager replies '£6 for every £1000 borrowed.'
Sally borrows £40 000 to buy the house.

What are her monthly repayments?

4 Copy and complete the following table.

Loan	Amount per £1000	Monthly repayment
£40 000	£6	£240
£28 000	£6	
£53 000	£8	
£71 000	£8	
£37 500	£10	

CHECK-UP ON BANKING MONEY

1 Andy has just written a cheque to Scot Fuel for £54.32.
Here is the cheque stub.

Date:	*17/12/95*
To:	*Scot Fuel*
Balance Bt. Fwd:	*£216.90*
This cheque:	*£54.32*
Balance:	

Calculate the balance.

2 Sylvia has a balance of £87 in her current account.
She writes cheques for
   £16 for petrol,
   £25 for shoes and
   £18.55 for groceries.

How much money has she left in her current account?

3 Calculate:
a 5% of £40 **b** 8% of £75.

4 Calculate the interest on £200 at 5% p.a.

5 Copy this extract from a bank book and fill in the interest and final balance.

REGAL BANK
Deposit Account Interest Rate
6% p.a.

Date	Code	Deposit	Debit	Balance
28/6/95	Cash	£250		£250
28/6/96	Interest	?		?

6 a Copy this machine and calculate the interest.

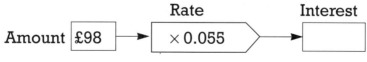

Amount £98 → × 0.055 → [Interest]

b Copy this machine to calculate the balance.

Amount £160 → × 1.085 → [Balance]

7 Sue and Carl want to buy a house which costs £85 000.
The bank manager offers them a 95% loan.

How much will they have to pay as a deposit?

8 A bank offers 85% loans.

   a What **percentage** must be found as a deposit?
   b What is 85% of £60 000?

9 This table shows the monthly repayments on a loan of £1000 for different rates of interest and for differing lengths of time.

To borrow £1000			
Period of loan	**Interest rates**		
Months	8% £	9% £	10% £
12	77	77.50	78
24	35	35.70	36
36	21	21.80	22
42	17.30	17.80	18
48	14.40	14.90	15.40

Find the monthly repayments on:

   a £1000 at 8% for 12 months   **b** £6000 at 8% for 12 months
   c £1000 at 10% for 36 months   **d** £5000 at 10% for 36 months.

10 STATISTICS AND PROBABILITY

LOOKING BACK

1

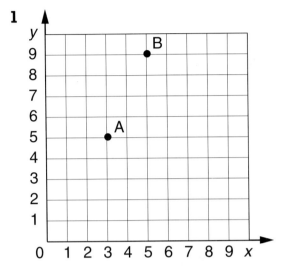

Copy this diagram on squared paper.
a Plot the points C(1, 1), D(2, 3) and E(4, 7).

b Give the coordinates of the points:
  (i) A   (ii) B.

c What can you say about the five points on your diagram?

2 Sam graphed the height of a seedling over nine days.

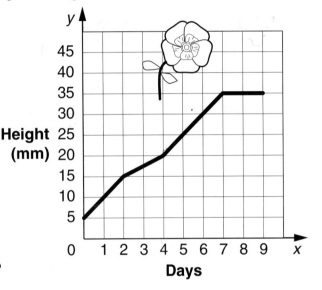

  a What was its height after four days?

  b When was it 30 mm tall?

  c The trend of the graph is 'the older the plant, the taller it gets'.
  When did the trend start to change?

3 Look at these two graphs.

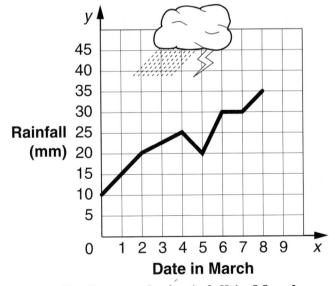

  (i) A record of rainfall in March

  (ii) How a £40 prize is shared out

a Describe the trend of each.

b In one day in March the rainfall went against the trend.
Which day was this?

113

$$\frac{1}{5} = 1 \div 5 = 0.2$$

4 Convert the following into decimal fractions:

   a $\frac{1}{2}$ **b** $\frac{1}{10}$ **c** $\frac{1}{3}$ (to 2 d.p.) **d** $\frac{1}{15}$ (to 2 d.p.)

5 There are 30 pupils in Daniel's class.

They were asked their favourite subject.

10 prefer maths.

2 prefer English.

15 prefer science.

3 prefer music.

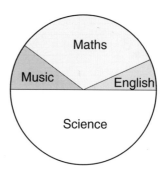

Maths
10 out of 30 = $\frac{10}{30}$ = 10 ÷ 30 = 0.33 prefer maths.

Repeat this step for the other subjects.

6

6 out of 10 cats prefer Kit-O-Kats

Write '6 out of 10' as:

  a a vulgar fraction

  b a decimal fraction.

Connections

When we graph two things which are related, there is often an easy **trend** to spot.

Examples

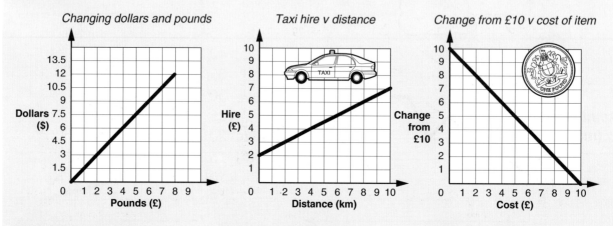

Dollars increase as pounds increase.
Dollars = 0 when pounds = 0.

A positive relation

Hire increases as distance increases.
Hire = £2 when distance = 0.

A positive relation

Change goes down as cost increases.
Change = £10 when cost = 0.

A negative relation

EXERCISE 1

For each of the following graphs:

(i)   describe the trend
(ii) give the *y*-value when the *x*-value is zero (see examples)
(iii) say whether the relation is positive or negative.

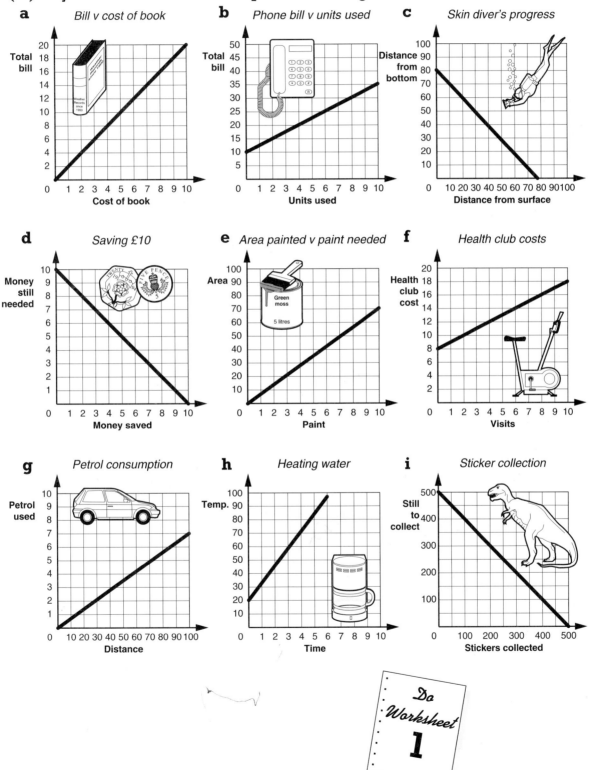

a Bill v cost of book

b Phone bill v units used

c Skin diver's progress

d Saving £10

e Area painted v paint needed

f Health club costs

g Petrol consumption

h Heating water

i Sticker collection

Do Worksheet 1

Loose Connections

Sometimes there is a connection, but it is not exact.
Here we see the lunchtime sales of ice-cream
at a café graphed against temperature.
The points lie roughly along a line.
The line suggests a **positive** relation.
The hotter the day, the higher the ice-cream sales.

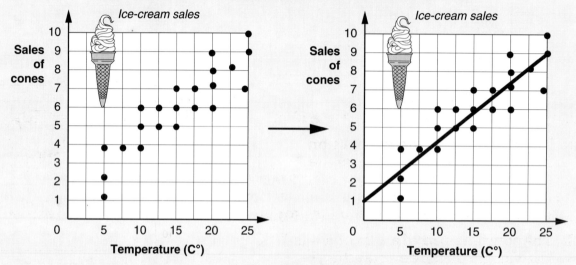

We can use the line to estimate sales.
For example, we could expect about three sales
on a day when it was 7°C.

EXERCISE 2

1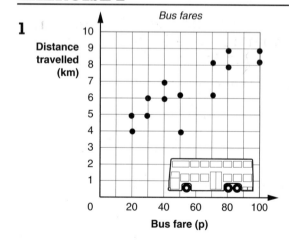

This chart suggests that the further you
want to go, the more you will pay.

a Is this a positive or negative connection?

b Use the chart to give a reasonable guess
at what a 7 km journey might cost.

c How far would you expect to go for
90 pence?

2 This chart suggests that the older the car,
the less you will pay.

a Is this a positive or negative connection?

b Use the chart to give a reasonable guess at
what a 3-year-old car might cost.

c How old would you expect a car to be if it
costs £6000?

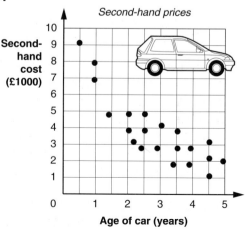

3

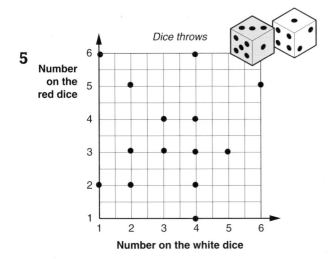

Gas bills

Heating cost per month (£) — vertical axis: 100, 90, 80, 70, 60, 50, 40, 30, 20, 10

Number of rooms — horizontal axis: 0, 2, 4, 6, 8, 10

The chart shows the connection between the number of rooms in a house and the heating costs.

a Is the connection positive or negative?

b Describe the connection in words.

c What size of bill might a 3-roomed house have?

4 Cups of tea were left standing at a fête.

a The chart shows the connection between the temperature of the tea and the time it has been standing.
   (i)   Is the connection positive or negative?
   (ii) Describe the connection in words.

b The temperature of a cup of tea is 70°C. How long has it been standing?

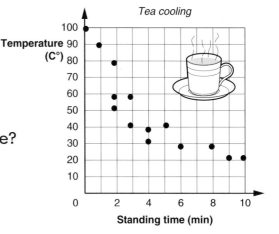

Tea cooling

Temperature (C°) — vertical axis: 100, 90, 80, 70, 60, 50, 40, 30, 20, 10

Standing time (min) — horizontal axis: 0, 2, 4, 6, 8, 10

5

Dice throws

Number on the red dice — vertical axis: 6, 5, 4, 3, 2, 1

Number on the white dice — horizontal axis: 1, 2, 3, 4, 5, 6

Two dice were thrown 14 times.

The chart shows the results.

Is there any connection between the number on the red dice and the number on the white?

Would you expect any?

6 Here are seven pairs of things. Say whether you expect a positive or negative connection, or no connection.

a A person's age and his/her shoe size.
b A person's life insurance and his/her age.
c A video's age and its rental cost.
d The distance you live from school and your maths mark.
e A car's age and its mileage.
f A person's height and the number of brothers he/she has.
g A person's maths mark and his/her science mark.

7 Name two things which have:
   a a positive connection   **b** a negative connection   **c** no connection.

Do Worksheet 2

Here is a table of exam marks:

Candidate	A	B	C	D	E	F	G	H	I	J
Maths mark	10	20	20	40	30	60	10	60	80	90
Science mark	10	10	20	30	40	50	60	70	70	90

... and here is a chart of the same.

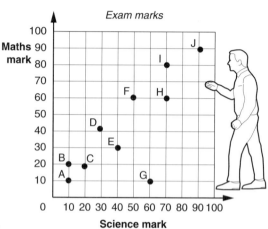

You can see:
- a positive connection between the maths and science marks
  (if you're good at maths you'll be good at science)
- candidate G goes against this trend.

EXERCISE 3

1 Ten pupils were given a general knowledge quiz.
   The table gives their ages and scores.

Candidate	A	B	C	D	E	F	G	H	I	J
Pupil's age	5	6	7	8	9	10	11	12	13	14
Score	10	20	40	30	10	60	50	80	60	90

   a Make a chart of the table.
   b Describe the connection between age and score.
   c Who goes against the trend?

2 Ten compact discs were studied.
   The table gives their average length of track and
   the number of tracks on each.

Disc	A	B	C	D	E	F	G	H	I	J
Average length of track (min)	2	3	3	4	5	5	6	6	7	8
Number of tracks	15	15	10	10	8	12	7	8	4	3

   a Make a chart of the table.
   b Describe the connection between track length
      and number of tracks.
   c Which disc goes against the trend?

3 Ten paintings were sold at auction.

Painting	A	B	C	D	E	F	G	H	I	J
Area of painting (m²)	1	3	4	4	4	5	6	7	7	9
Value (£1000)	10	2	8	5	7	1	5	9	3	4

Make a chart and see if there is a connection between area and value.

4 In a survey, the petrol a car used over 1 km was compared to its age.

Car	A	B	C	D	E	F	G	H	I	J
Age (years)	1	2	2	3	4	4	5	6	7	8
Petrol used (ml)	50	50	60	70	100	60	80	90	100	100

  a Make a chart.
  b Describe the connection between age and petrol consumpion.
  c Which car goes against the trend?

Do Worksheet 3

Remember the Likelihood Line

The numbers 0 to 1 can be used as a guide to how likely an event is.

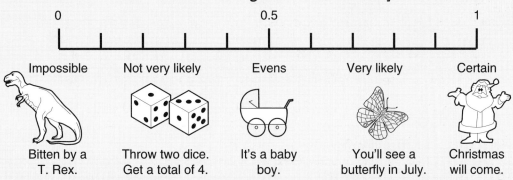

Impossible	Not very likely	Evens	Very likely	Certain
Bitten by a T. Rex.	Throw two dice. Get a total of 4.	It's a baby boy.	You'll see a butterfly in July.	Christmas will come.

Example   Jack wins if he throws a number less than 3.
There are six numbers on the dice. Two of these numbers are less than 3.

Two out of six are winners. $\frac{2}{6} = 2 \div 6 = 0.333$

We say: the probability of Jack winning is 0.333.

EXERCISE 4

1 Mandy wins the throw if she gets a number bigger than 3.
  a How many winning numbers are on the dice?
  b What is the probability that Mandy will win?

2 Jack and Mandy throw again if the dice shows 3 exactly.
  a How many threes are on the dice?
  b What is the probability that they have to throw again?

3 There are ten mugs.
Some of them contain a pea.
Jill wins if she picks a mug with a pea.

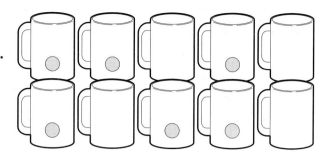

a How many ways can Jill:
(i) win (ii) lose?

b What is the probability that
Jill will win?

4

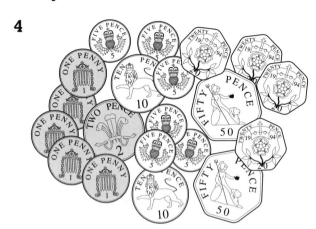

Hanif has 20 coins in his pocket.
He pulls one out at random.
What is the probability that it is:

a copper coloured

b round

c more than 10p

d 2p?

5 There are 500 balloons released in the balloon race.
200 are red. 150 are blue.
60 are green. 40 are yellow.
30 are orange. 20 are violet.
What is the probability that the
winning balloon will be:

a red **b** blue **c** orange or yellow?

Relative Frequency

Sam kept a record of the orders he took at the café.

Chips only	Egg and chips	Bacon, egg and chips	Bacon and egg only
~~HHH~~ ~~HHH~~ ~~HHH~~ ||| ~~HHH~~ ||||	~~HHH~~ ~~HHH~~ ~~HHH~~ |||	~~HHH~~ ~~HHH~~ ||	~~HHH~~ |
24	18	12	6

There were 60 customers that day.

24 out of 60 wanted chips only: $\frac{24}{60} = 24 \div 60 = 0.4$

18 out of 60 wanted egg and chips: $\frac{18}{60} = 18 \div 60 = 0.3$

12 out of 60 wanted bacon, egg and chips: $\frac{12}{60} = 12 \div 60 = 0.2$

6 out of 60 wanted bacon and egg only: $\frac{6}{60} = 6 \div 60 = 0.1$

These fractions are known as **relative frequencies**.

EXERCISE 5

1 Mike carried out a survey on pets. The results are shown in the table.

Dog	Cat	Fish	None of these
卌 I 卌 卌 卌	卌 II 卌 卌 卌	卌 III 卌 卌	卌 卌 卌 卌 卌 卌 卌 III
21	22	18	39

a Each person asked had only one pet.
How many people were asked?

b Work out the relative frequency of:
(i)   dog owners
(ii)   cat owners
(iii)   fish owners.

2 A company surveyed several people about toothpaste.
The table gives the results.

What toothpaste do you prefer?			
Dento	**Hygiena**	**Sensodent**	**Smiles**
12	8	40	20

a 12 people preferred Dento. How many preferred Sensodent?
b How many people were asked?
c Work out the relative frequency of each choice of toothpaste.

3 Mrs Smith had a good look at her phone bill.
She made a table of the length of the calls.

Length of telephone call				
Less than 2 minutes	**2 minutes**	**3 minutes**	**4 minutes**	**More than 4 minutes**
14	21	7	28	35

a How many calls were made?
b What is the relative frequency of calls:
    (i)   longer than 4 minutes
    (ii)   less than 2 minutes?
c (i) How many calls are less than
            4 minutes long?
    (ii) What is the relative frequency of calls
            less than 4 minutes long?

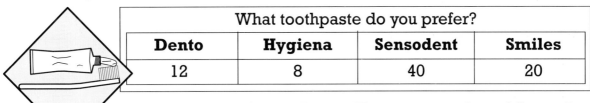

Do
Worksheet
4

Experimental Probability

If we take the results of a survey as typical of what will happen, then the relative frequency of an event can be taken as a measure of its likelihood.

Example
Kate had driven down the road 60 times.
She had been stopped by the red light 20 times.
What is the probability of being stopped by the lights?

The experimental probability of being stopped by the lights
$= \frac{20}{60} = 20 \div 60 = 0.333.$

EXERCISE 6

1 160 people were asked which colour of the rainbow they preferred.
The results are shown in the table.

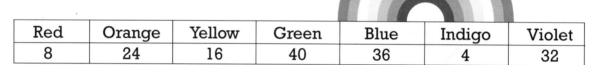

Red	Orange	Yellow	Green	Blue	Indigo	Violet
8	24	16	40	36	4	32

If these people are typical, what is the probability of picking a person who:

a prefers yellow   **b** prefers blue   **c** will not pick indigo?

2 100 householders were asked which emergency repair service they had called out most recently. Here are the results:

Electrician	Plumber	Joiner	Gas board	Slater
14	41	15	25	5

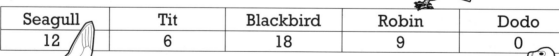

a How many called out the joiner?

b What is the relative frequency of calls to the slater?

c If these households are typical, what is the probability that the next repair service you'll need to call is:
(i) the electrician   (ii) the gas board?

3 Sam sighted 45 birds one day.

Seagull	Tit	Blackbird	Robin	Dodo
12	6	18	9	0

If this is a typical day, what is the probability of sighting:

a a seagull   **b** a robin   **c** a dodo?

CHECK-UP ON STATISTICS AND PROBABILITY

1 For each graph:
  (i) describe the trend
  (ii) say whether the relationship shown is positive or negative.

a

Distance v time

Time in flight (min)

Distance (km)

b

Bike hire

Cost of hire (£)

Hours hired

c

Thirst quencher

Amount drunk (ml)

Amount left (ml)

2 Examine each of the scatter diagrams below.

Scarf sales

Sales

Time after June

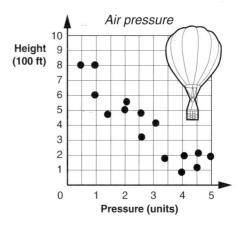

Air pressure

Height (100 ft)

Pressure (units)

Write a sentence about the relationship between:
  a the sales of scarves and the time after June
  b the height of the balloon and the air pressure.

3 Ten tennis players were asked how often they practised in the week.
They were asked to say how many matches they had won in the month.

Player	A	B	C	D	E	F	G	H	I	J
Number of practices in a week	1	1	2	2	3	4	4	5	5	6
Number of wins in a month	2	3	5	8	6	8	7	9	8	9

  a Make a chart of the table.
  b Describe the connection between practices and number of wins.
  c Which player goes against the trend?

4 A chess set contains 16 white and 16 red pieces.
The table gives how many of each type there are.

Rook	Knight	Bishop	Queen	King	Pawn
4	4	4	2	2	16

What is the probability that the first piece
out of the box will be:

a red   **b** a knight
c a pawn   **d** a king?

5 An ice-cream seller kept a record of lollipop sales.

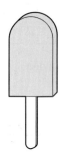
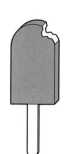

Orange	**Lime**	**Lemon**	**Raspberry**
卌 卌 卌 卌	卌 卌 卌 卌 卌	卌 卌 卌 卌	卌 卌 卌 卌 卌 卌 卌
20	25	20	35

Work out the relative frequency of:

a orange flavour sales
b raspberry flavour sales.

6

Distance from hole				
Less than 30 cm	**Between 30 and 50 cm**	**Between 50 and 100 cm**	**Between 1 m and 2 m**	**More than 2 m**
12	24	30	15	19

The table shows Bill's performance as he
chipped onto the golf greens.
For example, out of the last 100 chips,
24 landed between 30 and 50 cm from
the hole.
If the table is typical of Bill's play, what
is the probability that the next time Bill
chips a ball he lands:

a between 50 and 100 cm away
b more than 2 m away
c less than 50 cm away? (Be careful.)

11 WHAT DO YOU KNOW?

Bk 3 Ch 1, 6

WHOLE NUMBERS, FRACTIONS, DECIMALS AND PERCENTAGES

1 Copy and complete the crossword.

1	2			3
			4	
5				
6		7		
	8			

BODMAS

Across

1. $4 + 7 \times 19$

4. $\frac{1}{2}$ of $50 + 18$

6. $(322 - 2) \div 5$

8. $1 + 4 \times 25$

Down

2. $\frac{1}{2}$ of $(50 + 18)$

3. $11 \times (28 + 2) + 2$

5. $(6 + 14) \times 8$

7. $336 \div 6 + 4$

2 Round these numbers to the nearest whole number:

a 34.2   **b** 67.8   **c** 84.5   **d** 46.0

.5,.6,.7,.8,.9
up
.0,.1,.2,.3,.4
down

3  **a** Three friends share £2 equally.

How much does each person get?

b Peter orders taxis for 13 people.
A taxi will take a maximum of four people.

How many taxis will he have to order?

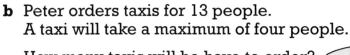

Be sensible!

4 The times of five cylists over a 100 metre dash were:
Adam 9.43 s   Bashir 9.39 s   Charles 9.5 s   Davie 9.06 s   Ed 9.12 s.

List the racers in the order they crossed the line.

5 Calculate:

a $\frac{1}{2}$ of 70   **b** $\frac{1}{7}$ of 56   **c** $\frac{1}{10}$ of 60

d 10% of 70   **e** 12% of 25   **f** 6% of 50

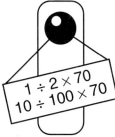
$1 \div 2 \times 70$
$10 \div 100 \times 70$

SCALES, TEMPERATURE AND TIME

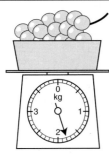

1 Janet weighs grapes in a container.

The weight of the grapes and container is shown on the scales.

The container weighs 0.5 kg.

How heavy are the grapes?

2 What is the volume of liquid in each measuring jug?

a  **b**

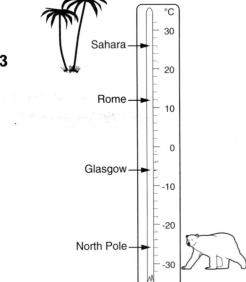

3 The scale shows the recorded temperatures of some places on one day.

a Name the four places and give their temperatures.

b How much warmer was Rome than Glasgow?

c It was 4° cooler in Paris than it was in Glasgow.
What was the temperature in Paris?

d It was 8° warmer in Siberia than it was at the North Pole.
What was the temperature in Siberia?

4 a Sam started work on the 8th of May and finished on the 24th of May. How many days did he work?

b Helen went on a cruise on the 24th of July and came back on the 12th of August. How long was she away?

c Ben started saving for a CD player on the 11th of February and finished on the 4th of April. How long did it take him?

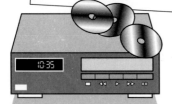

d SPONSORED CYCLATHON
Flo set out on the 21st of May. She finished on the 20th of July. How many days did it take her?

5 Niall has a six-hour videotape.
These programmes have been taped:

How many minutes of tape are left?

Horizon	50 minutes
Equinox	55 minutes
Dirty Dozen	150 minutes
Slightly Soiled Seven	40 minutes

6

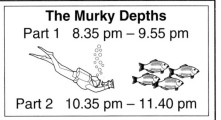

The Murky Depths
Part 1   8.35 pm – 9.55 pm

Part 2   10.35 pm – 11.40 pm

Sarah watches 'The Murky Depths' on TV.
It is shown in two parts, separated by the news.
a How long is the news?
b How long is: (i) Part 1   (ii) Part 2
(iii) the whole movie?

7

Arton	08 30	09 00	09 30	10 00	10 30	11 00
Beeton	08 35	09 05	09 35	10 05	10 35	11 05
Ceeton	08 47	09 17	09 47	10 17	10 47	11 17
Dayton	08 59	09 29	09 59	10 29	10 59	11 29
Eaton	09 15	09 45	10 15	10 45	11 15	11 45
Efton	09 29	09 59	10 29	10 59	11 29	11 59

Enjoy the journey – go by bus.

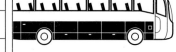

a How long is the journey fron Arton to Eaton?
b Matthew lives in Ceeton and has to get to Efton by 11 am.
What is the latest bus he can catch?
c Pat was in Beeton. He had just missed the 9 am bus from Arton.
When is the earliest he can arrive in Efton?

8

BBC 1		BBC 2	
5.30	Aussies at Home	4.35	Golf
6.00	Six o'clock News	6.10	**Film**: Stardust
6.30	Local News	7.40	University Challenge
7.00	The Antiques Show	8.30	The Wildebeast Show
7.30	Tomorrow's World	8.40	Daylight Sonata
8.00	Holiday	9.00	Whatever Happened to...

a Are these times am or pm?
b What is on BBC2 at 5 pm?
c How long does the BBC2 film last?
d Pete watches all of Tomorrow's World, then switches over to catch
University Challenge.
How much of University Challenge does he miss?

RATIO AND PROPORTION

Bk 4 Ch 2

1 Liz makes caramel shortcake.
The caramel is one part butter to
four parts sugar.

  a How many cups of sugar are needed
for three cups of butter?

  b How many grams of sugar are needed
for 100 grams of butter?

2   The Pedal-a-way Company charges £1.60 per hour
to hire a bike.

  a How much do they charge for an 8-hour hire?

  b How long do you get for £8?

3 At the March Hare's, tea for three costs £1.80.

At the same rate, what will it cost for:

  a tea for one   **b** tea for five?

4   **Happy Hols 10 days for £220**   **Happy Hols 12 days for £267**

The Simpsons want to rent a cottage
for their holiday.

Which is the better bargain?

You must show your working.

5 **£1 sterling = 2 Australian dollars**

  a How many dollars do you get for:

     (i) £2   (ii) £4   (iii) £1.50?

  b How many pounds (£) make:

     (i) $6   (ii) $10   (iii) $7?

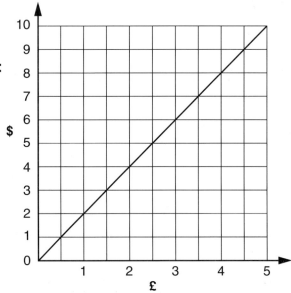

POSITION, SCALE AND BEARINGS

1

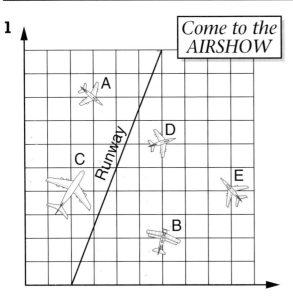

Come to the AIRSHOW

This is the map for an airshow.
The Avro (A) is at (3, 8).

a Give the coordinates of:

   (i)   the biplane at B

   (ii) the Comet at C

   (iii) the Dakota at D

   (iv) the Electra at E.

b The runway is represented by a line.
Give the coordinates of three points
on the runway.

2 Air traffic control notes
the bearings of the pilots.

Peter's is 110°.
George's is 060°.
Mary's is 260°.

a Who is flying:
   (i)   the Dakota
   (ii) the Avro
   (iii) the biplane?

b Helen is flying the Electra.
What is her bearing?

c The Comet is flying on a
bearing of 200°.
Between which two planes
is it flying?

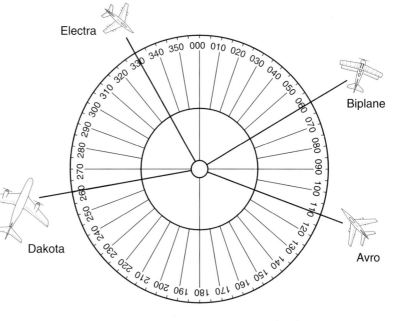

3

Length

Table   Stool

Wardrobe

Bed

This is a plan of Bryan's bedroom.

1 cm on the plan represents 35 cm.

a Use a ruler to measure the length
of the bedroom on the plan.

b Calculate the real length.

c How long is the real bed?

d A bookshelf is 105 cm long.
How long will it look in the plan?

EARNING, SPENDING AND SAVING

Bk 4 Ch 4, 7, 9

1 SALE
Was £65
Now £58.50

Super Train Set

Calculate the discount on the train set.

2 Calculate *A, B, C, D* and *E* to find out how much Mr Lowe has to pay for his electricity.

STANDARD ELECTRICITY plc				
B Lowe 23 Vapour St		18.07.96 – 20.10.96	Meter number 265312	
Meter Reading		Charges	Amount (£)	
Present	Previous			
38429	38001	*A* Units at 7p	*B*	
		STANDING CHARGE	9.10	
		Sub-total	*C*	
		VAT at 8%	*D*	
		TOTAL due	*E*	WE SHINE YOU SEE

3
Dinghy
£300
or HP Terms
Deposit £100
+
20 weeks at £12

a Calculate the cost of the dinghy on HP.

b How much cheaper is it to pay cash?

4 Dawn works at the Viking tourist centre.
She is paid £6.20 per hour. She works 35 hours a week.
How much is she paid per week?

5 Mike is a lighthouse keeper.
He is paid £7.50 per hour.
He is on duty 40 hours per week.
When he works over 40 hours he is paid double time.

How much is he paid in a week when he works 45 hours?

6 Sumitra is a sales person. She has a basic wage of £70 per week.
She is also paid 5% commission on her sales.
Last week she sold £5000 worth of goods.
a How much commission did she earn?
b What was her total wage that week?

7 You must pay 8% Value Added Tax (VAT) on your gas and electricity bills.

How much VAT do you pay on:
a a gas bill of £150
b an electricity bill of £200?

8 On most other items you pay 17.5% VAT.
This machine helps you to calculate the VAT.

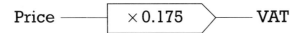

Price ——— | × 0.175 ⟩ — VAT

a Use the machine to calculate the VAT on:
   (i) £50   (ii) £650.

This machine helps you to calculate the price including VAT.

Price ——— | × 1.175 ⟩ — Price + VAT

b Use the machine to calculate the price plus VAT on:
   (i) £50   (ii) £650.

9

Date: *3/2/96*

To: *The Shoe Shop*

Balance Bt Fwd:
£ *£523*

This cheque:
£47.50

Balance:

£ _____

Sandy wrote a cheque to pay for some shoes. Here is the cheque stub.

a When was the cheque written?

b To whom was it paid?

c How much was the cheque for?

d What was Sandy's balance after the cheque was cashed?

10 Malcolm has a balance of £236 in his current account.
He writes these cheques:
£135 for groceries, £20 for petrol and £23 for a meal.
How much money will he have left in his current account?

11 Kirsty leaves £500 in her deposit account for a year.
The bank pays interest at 5% p.a.
How much interest does she get?

12 Austin and Ella want to buy a house which costs £90 000.

The bank manager offers them a 95% loan.

How much will they have to pay as a deposit?

LENGTH, AREA, VOLUME AND WEIGHT

Bk 3 Ch 12
Bk 4 Ch 5

1

Before

After

0 10 20 30 40 50 60 70 80
Millimetres

0 10 20 30 40 50 60 70 80
Millimetres

Jamie sharpened his pencil.
a How long was it: (i) before (ii) after he sharpened it?
b What length was lost?

2 km — x 1000 — m — x 100 — cm — x 10 — mm

Change:
a 3 km to metres **b** 12 m to centimetres **c** 7 cm to millimetres
d 1.5 km to metres **e** 12.6 m to centimetres **f** 8.4 cm to millimetres

3 Now change:
a 4000 m to kilometres **b** 500 cm to metres **c** 80 mm to centimetres
d 3400 m to kilometres **e** 320 cm to metres **f** 76 mm to centimetres

4

6 m

4 m

y

x

3 m

9 m

A carpet-fitter hammers a length of 'gripper' all round the room.

Calculate:

a the length of: (i) x (ii) y

b the perimeter of the room.

5 Each square represents one square centimetre (1 cm²).

a Estimate the area of:
(i) the circle
(ii) the leaf

b Work out the area of the triangle.

6 An artist has a canvas which is 40 cm by 50 cm.
  a What is the area of the canvas?

She paints a corner 30 cm by 10 cm.
  b What is the area of the corner?
  c What area is not painted?

7 Each small cube represents one cubic centimetre (1 cm³).

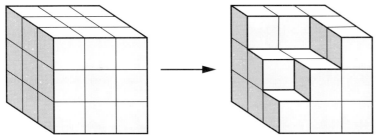

A large cube is made from the small cubes.
It then has some cubes removed as shown.

  a What is the volume of the large cube?
  b What volume has been removed?
  c What volume is left?

8 Megajuice is sold in cartons as shown.
What is the volume of the carton?

9 litres ——— ×1000 ——— ml

Change:
  a 3 litres to millilitres   **b** 6.2 litres to millilitres
  c 5000 millilitres to litres   **d** 7600 millilitres to litres

10 kilograms ——— ×1000 ——— grams

Change:
  a 5 kilograms to grams   **b** 7.1 kilograms to grams
  c 9000 grams to kilograms   **d** 2500 grams to kilograms

11

The McGregor family are off on holiday.
Each person is allowed 8.5 kg of luggage.

What total weight of luggage are they allowed?

SYMMETRY, ANGLES, 2-D AND 3-D SHAPES

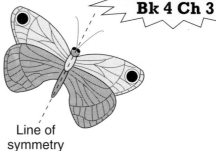

Bk 3 Ch 2, 7, 11
Bk 4 Ch 3

1 Copy and complete the pictures.
The dotted line is an axis of symmetry.

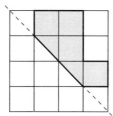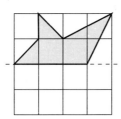

Line of
symmetry

2 Copy and continue this pattern.

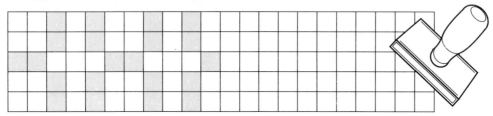

3

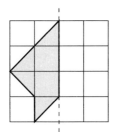

a Measure each of the labelled angles.

b What do you notice about p and r?

c What is the sum of the four angles?

p
s q
r

40°

4 Draw an angle of: **a** 40° **b** 150° **c** 210°.

5  **a** The diameter of the
10p coin is 2.6 cm.

How long is the radius?

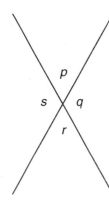 **b** The radius of the
penny is 1 cm.

What is its diameter?

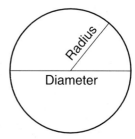

Radius

Diameter

6   The flag is rectangular.
Its height is 100 cm.
Its breadth is 220 cm

What is its perimeter?

100 cm

220 cm

7 A new stamp is designed. It is square. It has a side of 2.5 cm.

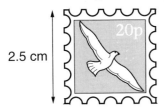

What is:
a the length of the stamp
b the length of the rectangle formed by three of the stamps
c the breadth of the rectangle?

8

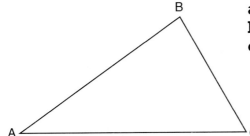

a Measure the angles of this triangle.
b What is their sum?
c Francis draws a triangle with angles of 65° and 70°.

What is the size of the third angle?

9 Here is an example of a square tiling.
Draw an example of how:

a a rectangle

b a triangle

might tile.

10 a Name each of the solids shown here.

b Name something which is sold in a container of each shape.

11 A toy company makes teepees.

The skeleton model shows its framework.

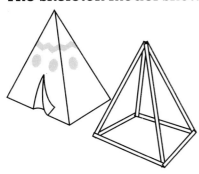

a A screw is needed at each vertex. How many are needed?
b The sloping poles are 2 m long. The horizontal poles are 1.5 m long. What total length is required?
c The net for the covering is started above. Copy and complete it.

PATTERNS, FORMULAE AND ALGEBRA

Bk 3 Ch 14
Bk 4 Ch 6

1 Find the next two numbers in these number patterns:

   a 7, 13, 19, 25, ..., ...   **b** 40, 43, 46, 49, ..., ...

2 The volume control is set at 2.
Danny shifts it h notches along.

  Which notch is it at now?

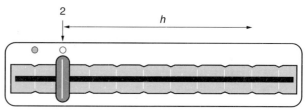

3 Simplify the following:

   a $2y + 3y + 4y$ **b** $x + 2y + 2x - y$ **c** $a \times 4 \times b$

4 If $x = 1$, $y = 2$, and $z = 3$, calculate:

   a $x + y + z$ **b** xy **c** $5z$

5 Find the unknown numbers in these equations:

   a $x + 2 = 3$ **b** $5 - a = 3$ **c** $6x = 18$

6 Historical Tours charge by using this formula:

> Number of pupils
> **times £3**
> **plus £5**
> gives the cost of party.

  The £5 is added as a booking fee.

  How much is charged for a party of:
  a 10   **b** 18?

7 A hardware shop sells hinges and screws.

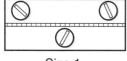
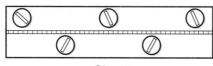
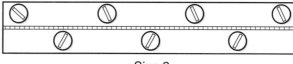

Size 1   Size 2   Size 3
3 screws   5 screws   7 screws

  a Make a sketch of what you think the size 4 hinge looks like.
  b Copy and complete the table.

Size number	1	2	3	4	5	6
Number of screws	3					

  c Write down a formula for finding the number of screws if the size is known.
  d The largest size hinge is size 10. How many screws are needed?

TABLES, CHARTS, GRAPHS AND STATISTICS

Bk 3 Ch 9, 10, 13
Bk 4 Ch 10

1

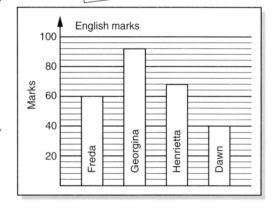

Paise

15	Elders
6	6	Howe
12	11	4	Stoon
12	18	12	7	Glass
18	24	18	13	6	Green

Distances in kilometres

a How far is it from Elders to Stoon?
b Calculate the distance travelled by a driver who goes from Paise to Stoon, then to Glass and back to Paise.

2 How many litres are equal to:

Changing pints to litres

Pints	Litres
1	0.57
2	1.14
3	1.71
4	2.27
5	2.84
6	3.41
7	3.98
8	4.55
9	5.11
10	5.68
20	11.37
30	17.05
40	22.73
50	28.41
100	56.83

a 6 pints
b 16 pints
c 60 pints
d 125 pints?

3 Four pupils sat a test.
It was out of 100.
The pass mark was 50.
The bar graph shows the pupils' marks.

a Who was top of the class?
b Who was second?
c Who failed the test?

English marks

Marks — Freda, Georgina, Henrietta, Dawn (100, 80, 60, 40, 20)

4 Paul drove his lorry between its depot and the delivery point.
  a How far from the depot is the delivery point?
  b Paul stopped for a mid-morning break.
    (i) How long was the break?   (ii) How far from the depot was he?
  c When did he reach the delivery point?
  d When did he arrive back at the depot?

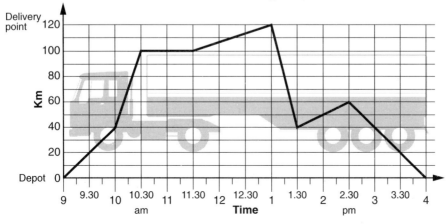

5 **a**

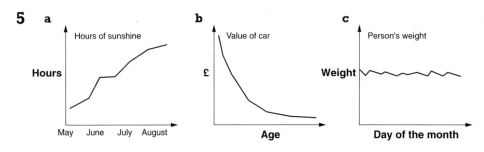

The above sketches of graphs show:

a the hours of sunshine over four months
b the value of a car as it gets older
c a person's weight chart over a month.

Describe the trend of each graph.

6 This pie chart shows what pupils did for lunch one day.

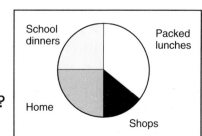

a What fraction had school dinners?
b What was: (i) least popular (ii) most popular?

7 Here is the rainfall recorded over ten days:
3 mm, 4 mm, 4 mm, 2 mm, 1 mm, 2 mm, 4 mm, 5 mm, 4 mm and 6 mm.
What was the average daily rainfall for this time?

8 **a**

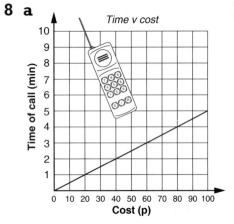

For each graph:

(i) describe the trend

(ii) say if the relation is positive or negative.

b

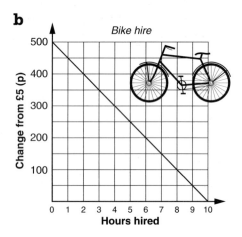

9 Examine each scatter diagram.

a

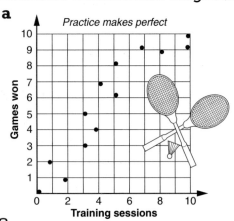

Say whether each relation is positive or negative.

b

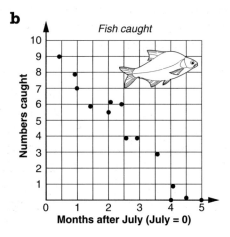

STRUCTURED DIAGRAMS AND PROBLEM SOLVING

Bk 3
Ch 3, 4

1 Jenny spins a coin three times.
She may get a head or a tail at any spin.

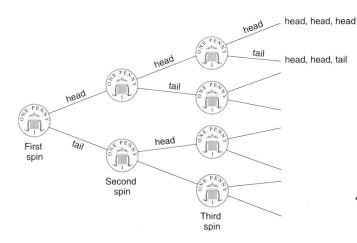

a Copy and complete the tree diagram.

b List the possible outcomes Jenny might have.

2 Jafar watched the traffic passing for ten minutes.
Some were cars.
Some had four doors.

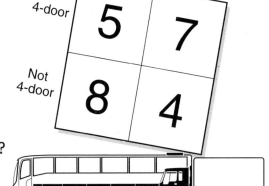

a How many 4-door vehicles were cars?
b How many cars were not 4-door?
c How many vehicles were not cars?
d How many vehicles passed Jafar?

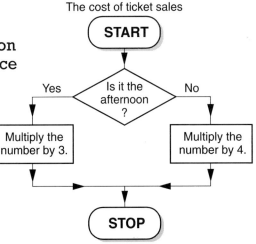

3

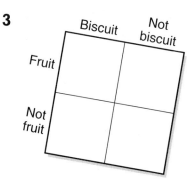

Ten pupils were asked about their packed lunch.

Five had a piece of fruit.

Five had a biscuit.

Three had both.

How many had neither?

4 A theatre runs two performances: an afternoon matinee for children and another performance in the evening for adults.

Tron Theatre

Evening £4
Afternoon £3

How much will it cost:
a four children in the afternoon
b three adults in the evening
c an adult and a child in the afternoon?

The cost of ticket sales

START

Is it the afternoon?

Yes — Multiply the number by 3.

No — Multiply the number by 4.

STOP

5 Make four straight cuts through the Christmas dumpling.

You must make 11 pieces only.

Each piece must have a 5p coin in it.

Guess and check

6 This shape is based on the Sphinx.

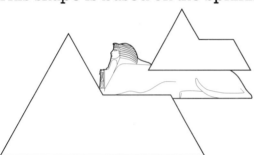

Make a model

Can you fit four small shapes into the big one?
(Use tracing paper.)

7 Four friends exchanged gifts at a Christmas party.

Angie gave to Cheryl.
Betty got the ornament.
Diane gave the gloves.
Cheryl did not get the scarf. No one gave a present to herself.
Who gave the chocolates?

Giver	Present	Receiver

Make a table

8 Pegs in a cloakroom are arranged as shown.

A simpler case

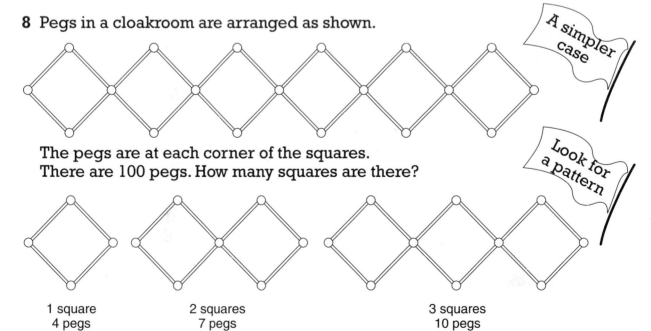

The pegs are at each corner of the squares.
There are 100 pegs. How many squares are there?

Look for a pattern

1 square
4 pegs

2 squares
7 pegs

3 squares
10 pegs

PROBABILITY

Bk 3 Ch 13
Bk 4 Ch 10

1 Here is the likelihood line. At one end is the word **certain**.

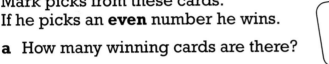

A   B   Certain

0 0.1 0.2 0.3 0.4 0.5 0.6 0.7 0.8 0.9 1.0

What word is usually found at:

a A **b** B?

2 Mark picks from these cards.
If he picks an **even** number he wins.

6 7 8 9 10

a How many winning cards are there?

b How many cards are there altogether?

c Mark will win 3 times out of 5.

Write the likelihood of his winning as a decimal.

d Draw a likelihood line and point out Mark's chances.

3 A survey of working dogs in a neighbourhood produced these results:

Collie	Spaniel	Labrador	German Shepherd
‖‖ ‖‖ ‖‖ ‖‖ ‖‖	‖‖ ‖‖ ‖‖ ‖‖ ‖‖ ‖‖	‖‖ ‖‖ ‖‖ ‖‖ ‖‖ ‖‖‖‖	‖‖ ‖‖ ‖‖ ‖‖ ‖‖ ‖
15	30	29	26

Work out the relative frequency of:

a collies

b German shepherds.

4 A sample of 36 screws was taken from a big box of mixed screws.
The table shows how many of each length were found.

Size of screw				
1 cm	2 cm	3 cm	4 cm	5 cm
6	3	9	8	10

If the table shows a typical sample, what is the probability that the next screw removed will be:

a 3 cm long

b more than 3 cm long?

12 MIXED REVISION EXERCISES

EXERCISE 1

1 Write down the answers to these:

    a 3.65×10 **b** $12.43 \div 10$ **c** 84.72×100 **d** $106.37 \div 100$

2 Round each of these numbers to the nearest 10.
(For example, 87 becomes 90.)

    a 38   **b** 23   **c** 97   **d** 121   **e** 285

3 **a** List all the **even** numbers between 1 and 15.
   b Which of the following numbers are **not** prime numbers?
      5, 9, 13, 21, 29, 35, 49

4 Bill, Younis, Alice and Dawn win £8 787 436 in the National Lottery.
They share it out evenly.

   a How much does each get?

   b Alice decides to give $\frac{1}{4}$ of her share to charity.

     How much does she give to charity?

5 The two dotted lines are axes of symmetry.

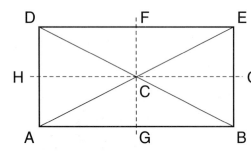

   Name:

   a a line equal to AD

   b three lines equal to DF

   c an angle equal to ∠ECB

   d three angles equal to ∠CAB.

6 Some students were asked these two questions:
'Do you watch any sport on TV?'
'Do you watch any cartoons on TV?'
The answers are shown in the diagram.

   a How many watch sport on TV?

   b How many do not watch cartoons?

   c How many watch sport but not cartoons?

   d How many students were asked?

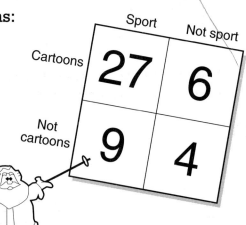

7 Tom, Becky and Ali have been measured. Their heights are shown beside the scale. What are the three heights?

8  The goals scored by United in their ten games so far this season are:
2, 0, 0, 3, 1, 1, 1, 0, 4, 3.

Calculate the **average** number of goals scored per game.

9  **a** The wheel has nine equally spaced spokes.

Calculate the size of each angle at the centre.

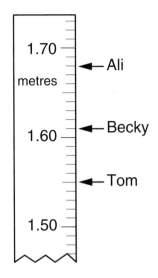

b Calculate the reflex angle at the centre of the cake.

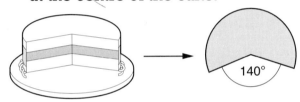

140°

10 Calculate the size of a and b.

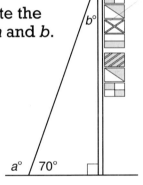

b°

a° / 70°

11 Amin's watch   Ben's watch   Clare's watch   Donna's watch

Ben's watch: 10:53   Donna's watch: 10:37

The right time is **twelve minutes to eleven**.
How many minutes fast or slow is each watch?

12 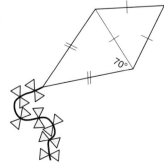 Gregor's kite is an equilateral triangle on top of an isosceles triangle.

70°

a Copy the kite.

b Fill in the sizes of as many angles as you can.

13 Find the next two numbers in each number pattern.

    a 3, 7, 11, 15, ..., ...   **b** 81, 72, 63, ..., ...

    c 3, 6, 12, 24, ..., ...   **d** 1, 2, 4, 7, 11, ..., ...

14 a Plot the points P(2, 1), Q(2, 5) and R(8, 3) on a coordinate diagram.

    b What kind of triangle is triangle PQR? How do you know?

    c Draw any lines of symmetry of the triangle.

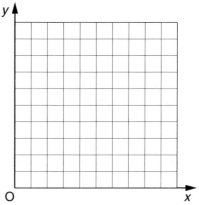

15

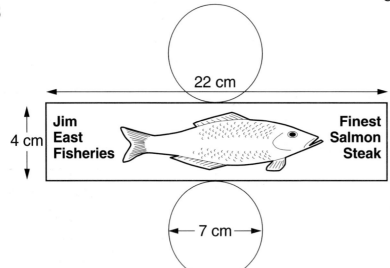

a Which 3-D shape does this net represent?

b What is the radius of the circles?

c What is the height of the shape?

16 Salek gets the job.

    a How much is he paid for a normal week of 35 hours?

    b One week Salek works 4 hours of overtime. How much is he paid for the overtime?

    c Next week Salek is asked to work 45 hours. How much should he be paid?

SITUATION VACANT
35-hour week
£4.20 an hour
Overtime is paid at double time

EXERCISE 2

1 These four tiles can be arranged to form 4-figure numbers.

    a What is the **largest** number the four tiles can form?

    b What is the **smallest** number you can make with all four tiles?

    c Write both numbers in words.

2 Round each of these numbers to the nearest 100.
(For example, 272 becomes 300.)
a 168 **b** 315 **c** 829 **d** 458 **e** 3462

3 a Use your calculator to work out:
(i) 5^2 (ii) 12^2 (iii) 20^2 (iv) 81^2

b Use your calculator to find which of
these numbers are **square** numbers:
(i) 64 (ii) 225 (iii) 200 (iv) 441

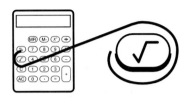

4 Zeta and Mardi buy materials to make Christmas decorations.
Copy and complete their bill:

```
3 rolls of sticky tape at £1.35 a roll
7 packs of gummed paper at 37p a pack
1 packet of cotton wool at £2.15
5 rolls of crepe paper at 68p a roll    _____

                          Total £  _____

RECEIPT ... WITH THANKS
```

5 Copy these shapes onto squared paper.

Complete the diagrams so that the shapes
have **half-turn symmetry** about the dot.

a   **b**

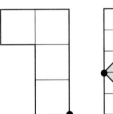
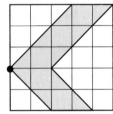

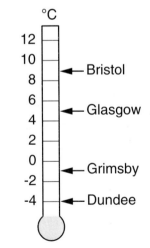

6

a Write down the temperatures of the four places.

b Which place is warmer, Grimsby or Dundee?

c Aberdeen is 5 degrees colder than Glasgow.

Write down the temperature of Aberdeen.

7 Measure these angles.

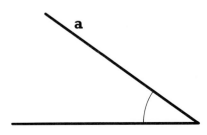
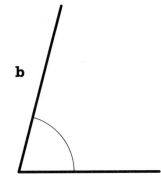
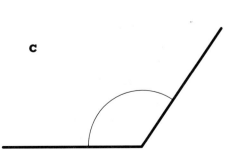

a   **b**   **c**

8 Calculate the size of each missing angle.

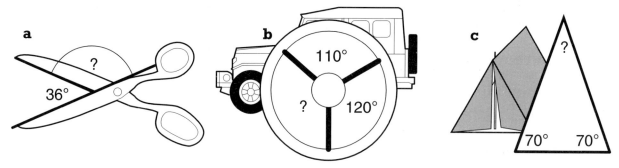

a ? 36°

b 110° ? 120°

c ? 70° 70°

9

NOVEMBER

a Copy and complete this page from a calendar.

b (i) How many Fridays are there?
   (ii) How many Mondays?

c On what day of the week is the 4th of December?

November						
S	**M**	**T**	**W**	**T**	**F**	**S**
				1	2	3
4						

10

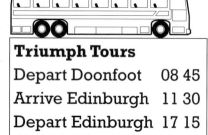

Doug drives a coach for Triumph Tours. One day he takes a party of tourists to Edinburgh and back.

Triumph Tours
Depart Doonfoot   08 45
Arrive Edinburgh   11 30
Depart Edinburgh   17 15
Arrive Doonfoot   19 45

a How long is Doug away from Doonfoot?

b How long is the drive:
   (i) to Edinburgh?   (ii) from Edinburgh?

c How long do the tourists have in Edinburgh?

11 Baljit decides to buy the music centre on hire purchase.

a Calculate the HP price.

b How much cheaper is it to pay cash?

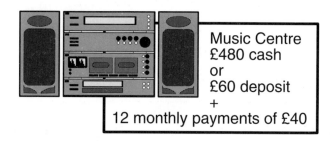

Music Centre
£480 cash
or
£60 deposit
+
12 monthly payments of £40

12

Anwar earns 2% commission on all his sales. One month he sells furniture worth £7500.

Calculate the commission he earns.

13 Susan Shaw's four gas bills for the year were:

spring   £58.75,   summer   £49.66,
autumn £84.92,   winter   £93.74.

What was her average gas bill?

14 a What 3-D solid does this net make?

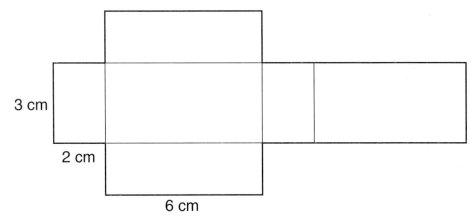

3 cm

2 cm

6 cm

b What is the volume of the 3-D solid?

15

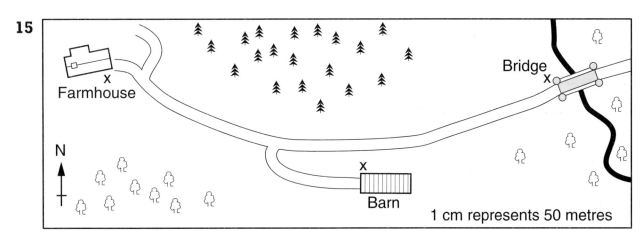

Farmhouse

Bridge

N

Barn

1 cm represents 50 metres

a Measure the distance on the plan from the farmhouse to:
   (i) the bridge   (ii) the barn.

b What is the actual distance from the farmhouse to:
   (i) the bridge   (ii) the barn?

EXERCISE 3

1 Calculate: **a** $2 \times 4 + 5$ **b** $2 + 3 \times 4$ **c** $6 - 3 \times 2$

2 Mark buys a tin of soup for 58p and a pizza for £1.65.

   a What is his total bill?

   b What change is he given from £5?

3 Mrs Creamer wants to buy 6 litres of milk.

NEWSTORE
1 litre carton 78p

BETTER DEAL
£1.42

SUPERSTORE
£1.96

a How much does she pay for 6 litres from Newstore?

b How much would she save by buying the 6 litres at Better Deal?

c How much cheaper is 6 litres in Superstore than in Newstore?

4 The diagram has half-turn symmetry.

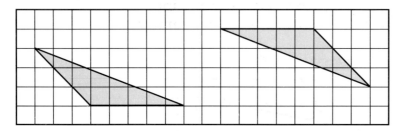

a Copy it onto squared paper.

b Find its centre of symmetry.

5  Workers at the Pie Place are given a pay rise.

The flowchart sets out the amount of the pay rise.

Calculate the new salary for workers earning:
a £5450   **b** £7250   **c** £12 380

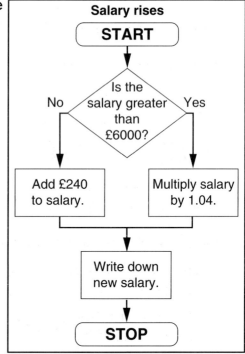

Salary rises

START

Is the salary greater than £6000?

No — Add £240 to salary.

Yes — Multiply salary by 1.04.

Write down new salary.

STOP

6  Debbie is paid £80 for stacking shelves.

$\frac{1}{5}$ of the money pays her rent.

$\frac{1}{4}$ of the money is spent on clothes.

She spends the rest on food and entertainment.

a How much is Debbie's rent?
b How much does she spend on clothes?
c How much does she have left for food and entertainment?

7 Which kind of angle is each of these?

   a 136°   **b** 85°   **c** 200°

   d 90°   **e** 95°   **f** 180°

8

Burns Hotel

June – September Full Board
ADULT PRICES
(per person)
1 night £48
2 nights £90
7 nights £280
Children half-price (up to 14 years of age)

The Burns Hotel advertises its new terms.

Mr and Mrs Pike and their two children, Paul (aged 16) and Polly (aged 13), go to the Burns Hotel for 7 nights.

Work out the family's bill.

9 Change these times to 24-hour times.

   a 7.45 am   **b** five past eleven in the morning

   c 4.05 pm   **d** a quarter to seven in the evening

10 Ahmed has built a ramp for his car. The side view is shown.

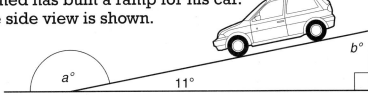

Calculate the values of a and b.

11 Country Taxis charge by using the formula:

The number of kilometres
times 40
plus 50
gives the cost in pence.

What is the cost of:

a a 3 km journey   **b** a 10 km journey   **c** a 15 km journey?

12 Sean and Caleb went hill-walking. The line graph shows their journey.

   a How long were they out on the hills?

   b How far did they walk before their first rest?

   c How long was the first rest?

   d How long did they **walk** altogether?

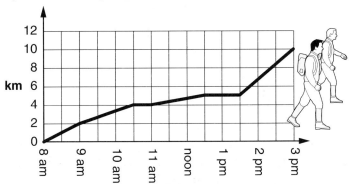

13 a Tara earns £24 for working a 6-hour day.
How much should she earn for working 8 hours?

b The ratio of girls to boys in a youth club is 3 : 1.
There are 36 members.
How many are boys?

14 Find the area of each shape.

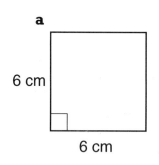   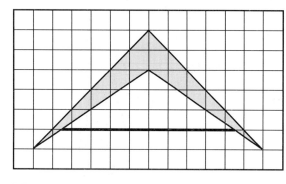   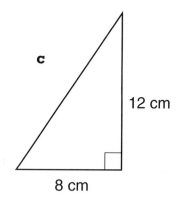

15 The diagram shows the logo for the Arden Aqua Club.

Make an enlargement of the logo so that its sides are all twice as long.

16 Fox's Fences pay their workers a summer bonus of 12% of their wage.
Calculate these summer bonuses:

a Henry, wage £140
b Lara, wage £220
c Winston, wage £250.

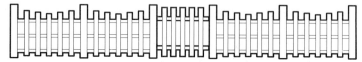

EXERCISE 4

1 Write the numbers in each list in order, lowest first:

a 9.06   20.6   19.95   8.88

b 3.17   3.07   3.1   3.7

2 15 balloons are to be shared equally among 6 children.

a How many balloons does each child get?

b How many balloons are left over?

3  Ali works in a fast food shop.
He is paid £3.85 an hour.
He works 37 hours.

How much does he earn?

4 (i) Copy each diagram onto squared paper.

(ii) Complete each so that the dotted line is an axis of symmetry.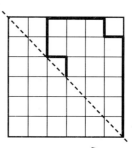

a

b

c

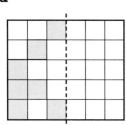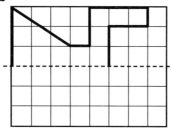

5 The numbers of visitors to a circus are shown below.

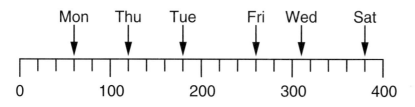

How many visitors were there each day?

6 There are 24 students in a class.
$\frac{1}{2}$ walk to school, $\frac{1}{8}$ take the bus, $\frac{1}{3}$ go by car, $\frac{1}{24}$ take a taxi.

a How many students take:
(i) the bus   (ii) a taxi?

b How many:
(i) walk   (ii) arrive by car?

c Check that all students are accounted for.

7 a Say whether each angle below is acute or obtuse.

(i)   (ii)   (iii)

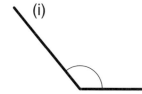

b Measure the sizes of the three angles.

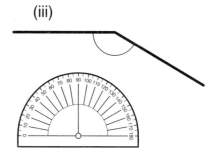

8 Calculate the size of each missing angle.

a

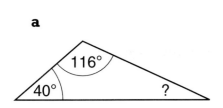

b

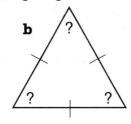

c

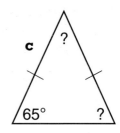

9 ABCDEFGH is a cuboid.

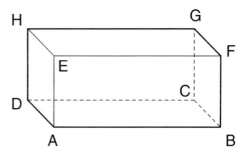

  a How many faces does it have?
  b How many edges?
  c How many vertices?
  d How many face diagonals are there?
  e How many space diagonals are there?
  Name one.

10

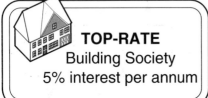

TOP-RATE
Building Society
5% interest per annum

Jason puts £400 into the Top-Rate Building Society.

  a How much interest will he get after one year?

  b How much money will Jason then have?

11 a On a coordinate diagram, plot the points K(1, 2), L(5, 8) and M(8, 9).

  b Draw kite KLMN.

  c Write down the coordinates of N.

12

E ○ E (E, E)
   ○ N (E, N)
   ○ S (E, S)

N

S

1st call

2nd call

Morag wishes to phone two friends, Alice and Bunty.
For each call, Morag knows three things could happen:

  ● the line may be engaged (E),
  ● there may be no answer (N),
  ● she is able to speak to her friend (S).

Copy and complete the tree diagram, listing the possible outcomes.

13 Three trains a day run from Drybridge to Galston.

	Train 1	Train 2	Train 3
Drybridge (depart)	07 15	16 00	21 30
Gatehead	07 35	16 35	21 55
Farm Loch	08 10	17 20	22 35
Galston (arrive)	09 00	18 25	23 35

  a How long does each train take to complete its journey?
  b How long does each train take to travel from Gatehead to Farm Loch?

14  Gary can't remember the combination of his padlock.
He knows there is a 3, a 6 and a 7.
He tries 367 but it doesn't work.

Make a list of all the other possible combinations.

15 A new adventure toy is produced. It has large linking boxes with windows.

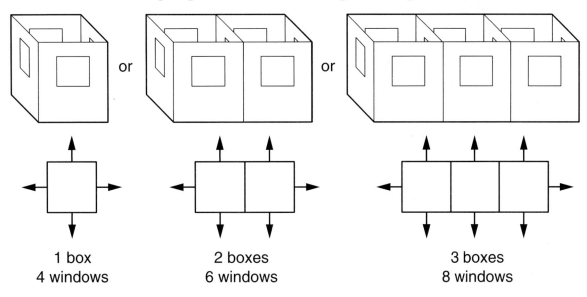

or   or

1 box   2 boxes   3 boxes
4 windows   6 windows   8 windows

a Make a sketch of the arrangement for four boxes.

b Copy and complete the table:

Number of boxes	1	2	3	4	5	6
Number of windows	4					

c Write down a formula for finding the number of windows
if the number of boxes is known.
Write it in the form: 'The number of windows is equal to …'.

d How many windows are in ten joined boxes?

16 A group of 36 people were asked what they
would buy first if they won the Lottery.
The results are shown in the pie chart.

a What is the first thing most would
spend money on?

b What was the least popular choice?

c What fraction would buy a car first?

d How many would buy a car first?

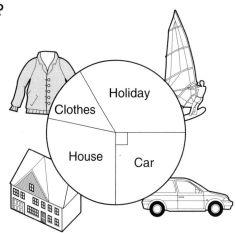

EXERCISE 5

1 Fatima ran six 100 metre races in training.
Her times in seconds were:
15.01, 14.8, 14.75, 14.95, 15.23, 14.82.

    a Write her times in order, fastest first.
    b What was her total time for the six races?
    c What was her average time?

2 **a** List the first six odd numbers.
    b List four prime numbers between 10 and 20.

3 Esther is paid £158.75 for 38 hours of work.
How much does she earn per hour? (Answer to the nearest penny.)

4

    a What is the weight of the bowl?

    b What is the weight of the bowl plus fruit?

    c What is the weight of the fruit?

5 Train fares are to rise by 10%.
What will the increase be on these fares?
    a £3   **b** £6.50   **c** £12.42

6 Torin has a new 4-hour videotape.
He tapes these three programmes.

How much time is left on the tape?

Holiday Snaps	45 minutes
Learn Spanish	50 minutes
Movie Show	1 hour 50 minutes

7 Newspapers advertise to make money.
The Barassie Bugle's charges are as follows.

Less than 10 words	20p per word
10 words to 20 words	18p per word
More than 20 words	15p per word

Calculate the cost of placing these three adverts.
(Each underlined part counts as a word.)

a
Ford Fiesta
MOT till June 1994
Must be seen
Offers over £1500
Tel. 61342

b
For Sale
Mountain bike
£120
Tel. 32661

c
For Sale
Top quality enamel bath £1
Very good condition
Also
Plug for the above bath £180
Tel. 30301 after 6pm on Saturdays

8 Draw an angle of:

a 55°   **b** 105°

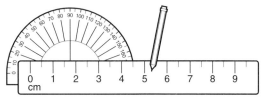

9 The front of this house is made up of an equilateral triangle on top of a square.

Write down the size of the angles at *a* and *b*.

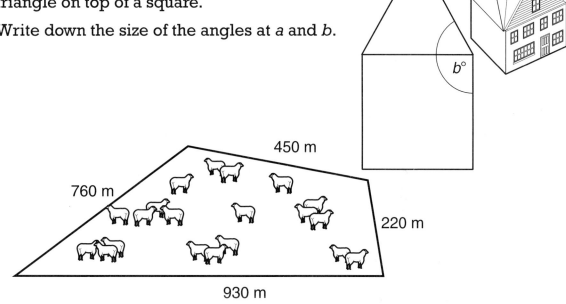

10

450 m

760 m

220 m

930 m

a Calculate the perimeter of the farmer's field in metres.
b Give the answer in kilometres.

11 a On a coordinate diagram, plot the points A(3, 1), B(7, 1) and C(7, 5).

b Draw square ABCD and write down the coordinates of D.

c Draw the diagonals.

d Write down the coordinates of the point where they cross.

12

a 12 bags of crisps cost £2.76. How much should 10 bags of the same crisps cost?

b The tuck shop keeps plain and tomato flavours of crisps.
The ratio of plain to tomato is 1 : 5.
If the shop has 78 bags of crisps altogether, how many bags are plain?

13 Malik makes £10 profit from selling 20 magazines.

How much profit will he make from selling 30 magazines?

14

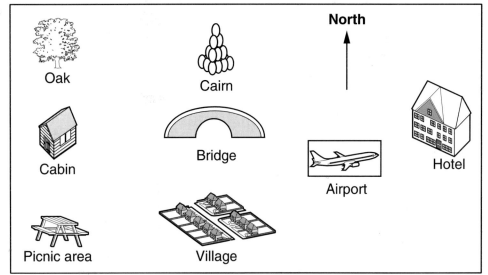

North

Oak

Cairn

Bridge

Airport

Hotel

Cabin

Picnic area

Village

a The cairn is north of the bridge in the diagram.
In what direction from the bridge is:
(i) the hotel   (ii) the picnic area?
b In what direction is the hotel from the village?
c Estimate the 3-figure bearing from the cairn of:
(i) the hotel   (ii) the village   (iii) the picnic area.

15 Copy and complete Mrs Ring's electricity bill.

SPARKS ELECTRIC PLC

Mrs Ring, The Stables		12.03.97–15.06.97		Amount (£)
Meter Reading				Amount (£)
Present	Previous			
23062	22895	A units at 8.35p		B
		STANDING CHARGE		£10.84
		Sub-total		C
		VAT at 8%		D
		TOTAL to pay		E

16 Jess borrows £3000 from Easy Loan to pay for her new car.
For the first year of the loan, Jess is charged interest at 28%.
How much interest is this?

17

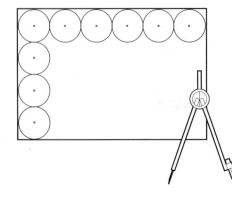

Linford can fit six of these circles
across his notebook.
The radius of each circle is 1.5 cm.

a What is the diameter of each circle?
b What is the length of Linford's notebook?
c What is its breadth?